May–August

Day by Day
with
God

Rooting women's lives in the Bible

15 The Chambers, Vineyard
Abingdon OX14 3FE
brf.org.uk

Bible Reading Fellowship is a charity (233280)
and company limited by guarantee (301324),
registered in England and Wales

ISBN 978 1 80039 123 9
All rights reserved

This edition © 2022 Bible Reading Fellowship
Cover image © iStock.com/kali9

Distributed in Australia by:
MediaCom Education Inc, PO Box 610, Unley, SA 5061
Tel: 1 800 811 311 | admin@mediacom.org.au

Distributed in New Zealand by:
Scripture Union Wholesale, PO Box 760, Wellington
Tel: 04 385 0421 | suwholesale@clear.net.nz

Acknowledgements
Scripture quotations marked with the following abbreviations are taken from the version
shown. Where no abbreviation is given, the quotation is taken from the same version as
the headline reference. NIV: The Holy Bible, New International Version (Anglicised edition)
copyright © 1979, 1984, 2011 by Biblica. Used by permission of Hodder & Stoughton
Publishers, a Hachette UK company. All rights reserved. 'NIV' is a registered trademark of
Biblica. UK trademark number 1448790. NKJV: The New King James Version®. Copyright ©
1982 by Thomas Nelson. Used by permission. All rights reserved. NLT: The Holy Bible, New
Living Translation, copyright © 1996, 2004, 2007, 2013. Used by permission of Tyndale House
Publishers, Inc., Carol Stream, Illinois 60188. All rights reserved. ESV: The Holy Bible, English
Standard Version, published by HarperCollins Publishers, © 2001 Crossway Bibles, a division
of Good News Publishers. Used by permission. All rights reserved. GNT: The Good News
Bible published by The Bible Societies/HarperCollins Publishers Ltd, UK © American Bible
Society 1966, 1971, 1976, 1992, used with permission. MSG: *The Message*, copyright © 1993,
1994, 1995, 1996, 2000, 2001, 2002 by Eugene H. Peterson. Used by permission of NavPress.
All rights reserved. Represented by Tyndale House Publishers, Inc. VOICE: The Voice Bible
Copyright © 2012 Thomas Nelson, Inc. The Voice™ translation © 2012 Ecclesia Bible Society
All rights reserved. TPT: The Passion Translation®. Copyright © 2017, 2018, 2020 by Passion &
Fire Ministries, Inc. Used by permission. All rights reserved. thePassionTranslation.com

A catalogue record for this book is available from the British Library

Printed and bound by Gutenberg Press, Tarxien, Malta

Day by Day
with
God

Edited by **Jackie Harris**   **May–August 2022**

Writers in this issue

Ruth Akinradewo's passion for Jesus underpins her advocacy for the marginalised, which she does through her involvement with three different Christian charities in the UK. Connect with her at **thechannelforchange.blogspot.com**.

Amy Boucher Pye is a writer, speaker and spiritual director who runs the *Woman Alive* book club. She's the author of several books, including *Celebrating Christmas* (BRF, 2021). Find her at **amyboucherpye.com**.

Selina Stone is tutor and lecturer in theology at St Mellitus College, where her teaching focuses on social ethics, Christian leadership and political issues. She has been writing for BRF for two years.

Caroline Fletcher is a freelance writer with a background in biblical studies. She lives in Sheffield and has been writing for *Day by Day with God* for the last three years.

Hannah Fytche is studying for her PhD in theology at the University of Cambridge. She has been a BRF author since 2015, when she wrote her first book, *God's Daughters*, and has been writing for *Day by Day with God* since 2018.

Cham Kaur Mann has over 25 years of leadership experience in the church, charity and voluntary sectors. She is the first (and currently only) Asian woman minister within the Baptist Union GB, and is co-director of Next Leadership.

Michele D. Morrison is a freelance writer, wife, mother and grandmother. She loves digging into God's word, listening for God's voice in the daily routines of life and blogging at **tearsamidthealiencorn.com**.

Rachel Ridler is mum to two energetic boys. She has used BRF's Parenting for Faith resources for many years and began writing for BRF in 2020. She loves exploring the Bible with others online, virtually and in person.

Victoria Byrne is married to Tim and is a lay pastor at St Stephen's Twickenham, leading ministry among older people. She has been writing for BRF since 2015.

Claire Musters is an author, speaker and editor with a passion for authenticity. Her most recent book (written with her husband) is *Grace-Filled Marriage*. Claire has been writing for *Day by Day with God* since 2012.

Welcome

Whether you have been part of *Day by Day with God* for many years or this is your very first issue, we're so glad you've joined us. We represent a diverse group of women – different ages, different backgrounds and with very different experiences – united by our love for God's word and desire to learn from it and draw strength and wisdom from it for our day-to-day lives.

In this issue, we welcome two new writers to the team. Ruth Akinradewo is a young Oxford graduate with a heart for those who are marginalised. She loves writing, music and singing, and begins our studies with one of her favourite characters – Esther. Later, we hear how Zelophehad's daughters, whose story is told in just a few verses in the book of Numbers, have continued to influence Cham Kaur Mann, who has many years' experience as a leader and mentor and is the first (and currently only) Asian woman Baptist minister.

It is always interesting to see how individual writers approach their topics and sometimes what they bring out of the same passage. In the course of our studies, two passages appear twice. The story of Jesus as a young boy – who left his parents without permission to spend time in the temple (Luke 2:41–50) – is referenced by both Selina and Rachel in their respective subjects, while Psalm 139 is used by Selina and then chosen by Ruth as her favourite psalm. Isn't it fascinating how God's word speaks to different people in different ways and at different times?

What is also interesting is how sometimes the same message can come through a variety of sources. We are exploring a wide range of topics, but as I read this issue through, a common theme seemed to emerge. In nearly every study there is something about God renewing and restoring, rewriting our stories, allowing new things to emerge or bringing something wonderful out of seemingly hopeless situations. Perhaps this is a message we need to hear.

Sometimes we forget that God's redeeming power can intervene in our lives, transforming situations, people and perceptions. As we study together over the next four months, may we hear God's word for us – a reminder of a promise, an assurance of his presence or a call to action – and draw strength and comfort from it.

Jackie Harris, Editor

Esther: seen *and* heard

Ruth Akinradewo writes:

Esther is an unusual book. Not only is it one of just two books in the Bible whose titles bear a woman's name (the other being Ruth), but it is also one of only two books in the Bible which do not mention the name of God (Song of Songs is the other). Oh, and where else do you find characters whose names begin with V, X and Z?

Perhaps, like me, if you hadn't been told, you wouldn't have noticed that this book does not explicitly reference God. But although his name does not appear, the story is clearly written by the hand of the creator. The young Jewess Esther is the pen that he holds to write the story; her older cousin Mordecai is the flowing ink whose help she cannot do without; and King Ahasuerus is the paper they must use to right the wrongs devised by the arch-enemy of the Jews, Haman.

Our God writes the best stories, and the book of Esther takes us masterfully through a number of different emotions. Who says God doesn't have a sense of humour? Haman is as fiendish as he is farcical. He reminds me of many a Shakespearean antagonist.

As is often the case with Shakespeare's plays, we know how the story of Esther will ultimately end. We know that good will triumph over evil. We know because 'if God is for us, who can be against us?' (Romans 8:31, NIV). Yet, though our Saviour promises us victory, he requires his children to be willing and obedient enough to fight in the battle he is leading. Esther is both. She starts off as a vulnerable young woman in a passive role, but when her people are threatened, she actively rises to their defence with courage.

Esther is one of my favourite characters in the Bible. She embodies what can happen when God turns things around. A woman in a man's world, she replaces a queen who is neither seen nor heard, but Esther makes herself both seen *and* heard, influencing the most powerful man in the kingdom to hang on to her every word. When we meet her, her heritage is exile and death. Her legacy for posterity? Togetherness – and *life*.

Esther and her courageous commitment to her people inspires me. I pray God speaks to you, too, in new ways as we learn from Esther together.

The kingdom starts at home

Now it came to pass in the days of Ahasuerus (this was the Ahasuerus who reigned over one hundred and twenty-seven provinces, from India to Ethiopia)… when he showed the riches of his glorious kingdom and the splendour of his excellent majesty for many days. (NKJV)

It is striking to me that the kingdom of King Ahasuerus – or Xerxes, as he is known in some versions – stretches over a range of ethnic groups. Contrary to the Eurocentric reading we often apply to the Bible, the book of Esther introduces us to a multicultural sphere where people of colour are in fact the majority. The story's setting is Persia (modern-day Iran), and Indians and Ethiopians feature too. With an array of peoples and tongues accounted for in the very word of God, we are reminded that the Bible is for *all* of us – just as God's kingdom is for all of us (Revelation 7:9).

King Ahasuerus clearly revels in the riches of his kingdom, which attest to his power. Giddy with his own acclaim (and wine), Ahasuerus fully expects his wife, Queen Vashti, to join the self-indulgence party he has been enjoying for a whopping 187 days already. She refuses.

I don't blame her for doing so: I certainly wouldn't want to parade in front of a bunch of drunken men! It is quite incredible that, despite being king over such a vast empire, Ahasuerus is incapable of effectively leading his own household.

Ahasuerus demonstrates what can happen to us when we focus more on status than we do on integrity. The king is so self-absorbed that he doesn't even see the problem with commanding his wife, whose beauty should be for him alone, to strut before a group of other men.

Our ministry, first and foremost, is to those closest to us. What does your family have to say about you? Your friends? Your local church? Even if you are revered the world over for your talents, if those closest to you have lost respect for you, your focus is probably in the wrong place.

Lord, help me to remember that your kingdom is for all, and that my most important role in it is to faithfully serve those closest to me with integrity – not to vie for everyone's attention. Amen

RUTH AKINRADEWO

A reversal of fortune

And Mordecai had brought up Hadassah, that is, Esther, his uncle's daughter, for she had neither father nor mother. The young woman was lovely and beautiful. When her father and mother died, Mordecai took her as his own daughter. (NKJV)

The story of Esther is full of reversals. Just like that, the deposition of Vashti and the coronation of Esther is complete (helped by some very poor advice). The reversals have only just begun.

Esther lost both her parents at a tender age. Though Mordecai took her in as his own daughter, he can do little to prevent the king's henchmen from bundling her off to the king's quarters as they please. Esther's face and figure will be pleasing to King Ahasuerus' eye – and so she is 'taken'. Just as Bathsheba had no say in being taken to King David's palace (2 Samuel 11), Esther is a woman subject to the orders of the king; she must simply follow instructions.

In modern-day terms, what happens to Esther and the other women in the harem is akin to human trafficking and sexual servitude. Esther starts off in obscurity and without a voice.

My dad died when I was 13, and during my childhood I suffered abuse. I can relate to the grief and powerlessness attached to Esther when we first meet her. Perhaps you can too.

The good news is that the story doesn't end there. Esther is promoted: her name becomes known throughout the empire and a feast is created in her honour. This is made possible because Esther wins over all who come into contact with her, gaining grace and favour. As followers of Jesus, we are called to walk in wisdom and speak with grace (Colossians 4:5–6), filling the air around us with 'fragrance' (2 Corinthians 2:14–15).

Esther reminds us of what can happen when God reverses our fortunes. He is in the business of rewriting our stories, beautifying the broken and removing shame – to clothe us with honour. We just need to be willing to be characters in his story of grace.

Father God, you are the redeemer of my past and my eternal Father. You have removed my shame and crowned me with victory. Help me to walk in your victory today, releasing your grace-filled fragrance to others. Amen

RUTH AKINRADEWO

The courage to stand

And all the king's servants who were within the king's gate bowed and paid homage to Haman, for so the king had commanded concerning him. But Mordecai would not bow or pay homage… for Mordecai had told them that he was a Jew. (NKJV)

Exposing the plan of King Ahasuerus' would-be assassins (2:21–22) could have been dangerous for Mordecai. What if the murderous eunuchs had caught wind of who had told on them before it was confirmed? Mordecai could have been dead meat!

Today's passage shows us Mordecai's consistent courage. He chooses to do the God-honouring thing, even when it could cost him dearly. He refuses to bow down to Haman, the king's second-in-command. Like Vashti in chapter 1, Mordecai cares more about integrity than the fragile ego of a self-absorbed man. His courageous resolve not to compromise reminds us of the actions of other exiled Jews in Persia: Daniel and his friends Shadrach, Meshach and Abednego (Daniel 1, 3, 6).

It's so much easier to fit in, isn't it? Standing on the Rock, the truth of Jesus and his word, is hard when everyone around you is sitting comfortably in the sand.

We live in a world where we are encouraged to bow down to ourselves. We can do whatever we like with our bodies, we're told. We can say whatever we want, however we want. But the gospel of Jesus isn't about self-indulgence; it's about self-denial – for the one who denied himself to save us for eternity. Will we be courageous enough to stand for him and be the odd ones out – even when the risks are great? Is there enough evidence to publicly 'convict' us of being Christians?

Mordecai is persecuted because his behaviour is distinct from those around him. Of course, his persecution is no small thing – with Mordecai's courage comes the legalisation of the extermination of all his people! Such evil is unlikely to come to us as Christians today. But today, you *will* have opportunities to stand boldly in your faith. Will you take them?

What would you have done if you had been in Mordecai's shoes? Ask God for more grace to stand boldly for him, even when it means you're the odd one out – and even when the cost is high.

RUTH AKINRADEWO

'If I perish, I perish!'

'Do not think in your heart that you will escape in the king's palace any more than all the other Jews. For if you remain completely silent… you and your father's house will perish. Yet who knows whether you have come to the kingdom for such a time as this?' (NKJV)

Esther reminds me of my favourite character in the Bible – which is Ruth (no surprises there!). Both Esther and Ruth (Ruth 1:16–17) speak and act with astonishing determination, inspired by dutiful love for their communities.

I love that Mordecai reminds his adopted daughter that just because she is a reigning queen doesn't mean she can forget her roots! He challenges her, 'Don't get too big for your boots! Do you think living in a palace makes you any less Jewish?' I find Mordecai's words amusing, yet full of daring truth.

As a black woman, I've experienced a fair bit of racism in my life. Yet despite the challenges I've faced, God has given me extraordinary opportunities – far more than I (or many with my skin colour) would imagine possible. Of course, I can't hide my skin colour like Esther could hide her Jewishness – but the challenge is the same: God does not elevate us simply for our own advancement.

As women, we live in a world where confines are systematically placed around us to limit the fullness of what God intends for us. When we break through these walls, God doesn't want us to replace them; he wants us to build doors to help others through.

It's important to remember where we came from – our progression doesn't make us better than anyone else. The ultimate example of this is to remember where *we* were before Jesus saved us. Now that we've been saved, we must extend a hand to others – to help save them too.

Helping others can be risky! Just ask Esther: her resolve to help her people could land her with a death sentence (4:11). Her bravery doesn't mean she is unbothered by that prospect – it shows that she loves her fellow Jews more than her own life.

Esther says, 'If I perish, I perish' (4:16). Appearing before the king to petition for her people could cost her life – yet she does it anyway. Ask God to give you Esther-like love for others – perfect love casts out fear!

RUTH AKINRADEWO

Haman: a lot of pride and a lot of falls

When Haman told his wife Zeresh and all his friends everything that had happened to him, [they] said to him, 'If Mordecai, before whom you have begun to fall, is of Jewish descent, you will not prevail against him but will surely fall before him.' (NKJV)

Today's passage is full of comedy gold!

We talked about reversals earlier this week – these chapters are full of them. Despite being elevated 'above all the princes' (3:1) by the king himself, Haman is still hung up on not getting the worship he wants from Mordecai. Talk about a fragile ego!

Mordecai, as an exiled Jew, is in both an ethnic and religious minority. We are told he sits within the king's gate, meaning he likely worked for King Ahasuerus – perhaps as a porter or guard. He's dispossessed of Haman's power. Yet Haman's joy at being invited to dine with the royals turns into 'rage' (NIV) simply because Mordecai does not 'tremble before him' (NKJV).

It is dangerous to root our identity in how others perceive us. The opinions of others are changeable – and not everyone will cheer us on. But our Father God calls us his children (1 John 3:1). Like a monarch bestows titles upon their relatives, the king of the universe calls us 'a *chosen* generation, a *royal* priesthood… his own special people' (1 Peter 2:9, my emphasis). The opinions of everyone else don't matter nearly as much!

Honour from the king wasn't enough for Haman – and thus began his downfall. 'Pride goes before destruction, and a haughty spirit before a fall' (Proverbs 16:18). Just imagine Haman's face as he led Mordecai through the city in the kingly array he'd dreamed up for himself!

Through God's divine orchestration, Mordecai is honoured for his loyalty to the king – albeit some four years later. In that time, Mordecai does not seek praise, but humbly and dutifully continues in service. Haman could have learnt a lot from him. Instead, he ends up in a heap at Queen Esther's feet – and hanged from the very gallows he had built for Mordecai.

Do you care more than you'd like about the opinions of others? Ask God to root your identity securely in him: 'Those who exalt themselves will be humbled, and those who humble themselves will be exalted' (Luke 14:11, NIV).

RUTH AKINRADEWO

Signed, sealed, delivered

Now in the twelfth month… on the thirteenth day, the time came for the king's command and his decree to be executed. On the day that the enemies of the Jews had hoped to overpower them, the opposite occurred, in that the Jews themselves overpowered those who hated them. (NKJV)

There are a number of turnarounds in this passage before the ultimate one. The king gifts Queen Esther with Haman's estate. Mordecai, whose true identity was earlier unknown to the king, is now welcomed to the palace as King Ahasuerus' in-law. He is given the signet ring which Haman once wore.

Esther's manner towards the king changes, too. Where she previously requested the deliverance of her people with decorum and restraint, she now pleads for the Jews with tears falling down her face, and herself falling to the king's feet. Where Haman stood as he begged for his life, only to fall (7:7–8), Esther first falls humbly, and then the king invites her to stand (8:4). What confirmation that God exalts those who first humble themselves!

Even when Esther has the king's ear, she makes her request with incredible deference. (Ahasuerus likes his ego stroked.) Have you noticed that when you ask for something politely, you're more likely to get a positive response? Esther's approach isn't manipulative, but wise.

Ahasuerus isn't one for actioning anything himself though – he has his officials for that! This time, the Esther-Mordecai duo take matters into their own hands, with his blessing. And so the counter-decree allowing the Jews to destroy their would-be destroyers is signed, sealed and delivered. The glorious news is dispatched with urgency.

We all have been issued with a life-saving counter-decree: the gospel of Jesus. It revokes the death sentence we were born under (Romans 6:23) and equips us to destroy the ultimate destroyer (John 10:10). The decree is signed by God with the blood of Jesus. His signet ring – the cross – seals it. His fingerprint of grace is all over it. We are the couriers who must urgently send out the good news. Signed, sealed, delivered – we're his!

How does today's passage make you feel? Have you ever considered the gospel as a counter-decree, reversing your fate? Ask God to fill you with a sense of urgency to deliver the good news of eternal salvation to others today.
RUTH AKINRADEWO

Remember, remember

The Jews established and imposed it upon themselves and their descendants and all who would join them, that without fail they should celebrate these two days every year, according to the written instructions and according to the prescribed time, that these days should be remembered. (NKJV)

We humans are so quick to forget, aren't we? We see it time and again in the scriptures: no sooner have the Israelites been rescued from impending disaster than they start moaning again!

Esther and Mordecai were determined not to let collective amnesia arise again. Though his name isn't mentioned once in the book of Esther, we can be sure that the Jews knew that God had ordained their triumphant rescue. The king gave them permission to slaughter over 75,000 anti-Semites who wanted them dead – finishing a war that had begun in the time of King Saul (1 Samuel 15). Their sorrow, weeping and wailing in the face of looming extermination turns into joy, levity and laughter. Fasting turns into feasting. They rest from their hard-fought victory and give gifts to one another. That's a lot of reversals!

As we learned earlier in this study, it's important for us to remember where God has brought us from. It not only keeps us humble, but also reminds us that God is faithful to his people (Romans 8:28).

Even in its very name, the festival of Purim reminds Jewish people today that God reversed their fate (*pur* comes from the lot that Haman cast in the Jews' *dis*favour). We, as Christians, are exhorted to remember Jesus' crucifixion; it reminds us that God reversed our fate and gave us victory over the enemy – that's cause for celebration!

It doesn't matter how our enemies throw the dice: our Father has the final say (Proverbs 16:33). He gives everyone free will, but he will use even the wicked to accomplish his purposes. He's the God who elevates a young, orphaned Jewess to the position of queen over a kingdom – and uses her to save her entire race. He can use you too. That's worth remembering.

Father God, help me to remember that you are faithful to your people. You elevated Esther and Mordecai, and you can use me to accomplish your purpose, too. May I continue to learn from the life of Esther. Amen

RUTH AKINRADEWO

Life in the garden

Amy Boucher Pye writes:

As we begin a fortnight of digging into the theme of gardens in the Bible, I want to confess my imposter syndrome related to this topic. I'm just not much of a gardener – which you'd see straight away if you came to tea in our vicarage garden. The beds that we cleared last autumn are now bursting with weeds. Spread across the lawn are the feathers of a bird who probably lost her battle with a fox. One of the pots I left out over the winter has cracked, its pieces scattered below it. Yet even in the mess, the daffodils and forsythia spread their cheer through their bright yellow flowers, catching my eye when I glance out of my study window.

Perhaps my vicarage garden gives a realistic view of life east of Eden. We no longer live within that safe and verdant space that Adam and Eve enjoyed with God, naked and unafraid. Now we have to deal with foxes in the garden and weeds growing apace – but even in the mess we can enjoy flashes of colour and beauty.

This theme will take us from Genesis to Revelation, for God sets his first people in a garden and, at the end of time, God promises to take us to his holy city in paradise, where we will enjoy life in a garden. We will explore how Israel longed to return to the garden of the Lord as they looked back to Eden, including some beautiful imagery from the Psalms and the Song of Songs.

As we move to the New Testament, we will see how Jesus spent some key moments in gardens. For instance, he spoke on the night he was betrayed about being the vine and his Father the gardener, before pouring himself out in prayer to his Father in the garden of Gethsemane. And then after he died, the garden became an amazing place when he appeared there to Mary – he had risen from the dead and was alive! Finally we end with passages from Revelation and the glorious tree of life planted by the river flowing from God.

I pray you'll receive much encouragement and grace from God as we ponder this garden imagery, and praise the one who created us and through whom we bear fruit.

The master gardener

Now the Lord God had planted a garden in the east, in Eden; and there he put the man he had formed. (NIV)

Have you ever noticed how God formed the heavens and the earth, calling them and all that filled them into being, but that he *planted* 'a garden in the East, in Eden' (v. 8)? And how he held off setting into motion the shrubs and plants until he had made someone to care for them (vv. 5, 7)? Only after he'd created Adam did he plant the garden and there put 'trees that were pleasing to the eye and good for food', alongside the tree of life and the tree of the knowledge of good and evil (v. 9).

Although I am not much of a gardener, I have the potential to become one – simply because God is a gardener and I'm made in his image. Tending the garden symbolises the work God calls us to do in partnership with him. Before Adam and Eve turned in disobedience against God, he invited them to work the land and tend the plants. For God, work was always part of his master plan of how those made in his image would exercise their creativity, insights and passions.

We don't know how it would feel to work without toil, but I suspect we've all experienced moments when we're in the flow of what we feel we've been made to do, whether it's when a child we're teaching has an 'a-ha' moment, when we help supply the necessary data to create a world-changing vaccine (as one of my friends did), or when we sit in our garden at the end of a warm spring day, sipping something cold and revelling in the artistry we've helped to cultivate.

What gardening – however you interpret that term – can you do today?

Creator God, thank you for forming me in your image. Help me to create in partnership with you, spreading truth and beauty in my patch of the earth. Amen

AMY BOUCHER PYE

Thorns and thistles

The Lord God banished him from the Garden of Eden to work the ground from which he had been taken. After he drove the man out, he placed on the east side of the Garden of Eden cherubim and a flaming sword. (NIV)

A child caught in the act of wrongdoing might try to bluster their way out of the situation, but soon (I hope) they will confess their actions. When the denials happen with our kids, I always wonder how long this stage will continue; when at last their countenance changes to sorrow, I breathe a sigh of relief.

I wonder what God felt when he found Adam and Eve hiding from him, shame having entered the world. Adam blamed Eve, Eve blamed the serpent and God had to deliver the news of the curse that came from them eating of the tree of the knowledge of good and evil: Eve's desire would be for her husband and he'd rule over her; Adam's work would now be filled with toil and travail, the ground unyielding and boasting of thorns and thistles. Our first parents were banished from the garden of Eden, kept out by a flaming sword and cherubim (vv. 23–24).

The rest of the Bible's story grapples with this sorry state of affairs. But as we know, God hasn't left his people to suffer without hope or rest. As we'll explore, he recreates flashes of his original garden for his people to enjoy. With him they – that is, we – usher in his kingdom through the sacrificial work of his Son Jesus.

Take some time in nature today, whichever bits are available to you, even if that's just looking up into the sky. Ask God as you ponder his goodness and greatness to reveal to you your heart, and any sins you may need to confess to him. May we continue to be pliable and tender towards God our maker.

Lord God, I've sinned against you, in thought, word and deed. Cleanse the thoughts of my heart by the inspiration of your Holy Spirit, that I may love and serve you. Amen

AMY BOUCHER PYE

Living in Sodom

Lot looked around and saw that the whole plain of the Jordan towards Zoar was well watered, like the garden of the Lord, like the land of Egypt… So Lot chose for himself the whole plain of the Jordan and set out towards the east. (NIV)

After God extended a covenant to Abram, to make his name great and to bless him (Genesis 12:2–3), he made good on that promise. So much so that as Abram and his nephew Lot worked the land, divisions started to arise between their herdsmen. For both to continue to flourish, Abram offered to Lot the choice of going to the left or to the right, saying he'd go in the opposite way. As we see, Lot chose to ignore the reputation of Sodom; instead, he was tempted by the well-watered land, which appeared 'like the garden of the Lord' (v. 10).

Lot hankered after what appeared to be fertile land, reminiscent of Eden. It may have been rich soil, but the inhabitants were evil and soon Lot got caught up in the skirmishes between kings. Because he was 'living in Sodom' (Genesis 14:12), he and his possessions were captured, and Abram had to come to his rescue. The life Lot had envisioned hadn't come to fruition.

How often do our choices reveal that we too have been 'living in Sodom'? We might, like Lot, have ignored the nudge in our spirit over some choice as we instead barrel ahead. Or maybe we weighed up what we saw as the facts and decided that we could withstand the evil we might face. Perhaps we find ourselves captured and in need of help.

We have a rescuer: God, who sent his Son Jesus to walk among the thistles and to provide us with living water. He saves us from our poor decisions – and he helps us to make wiser ones in the future.

Compassionate God, thank you for your love; thank you that you rescue me when I turn from you. Help me to depend on you, looking to you for wisdom and help. Amen

AMY BOUCHER PYE

Fruit in season

That person is like a tree planted by streams of water, which yields its fruit in season and whose leaf does not wither – whatever they do prospers. (NIV)

Perhaps I'm too focused on the short-term to enjoy gardening. I know that if I want to enjoy the autumn harvest, I have to work hard in the spring and summer. But after the winter passes, I don't relish having to clear the weeds – I too often prefer taking a walk along the nearby brook, enjoying the wild garlic springing to life.

But as Psalm 1 makes clear, trees planted by streams of water will bear fruit 'in season'; their leaf 'does not wither – whatever they do prospers' (v. 3). The psalmist uses this rich language to point towards the benefits afforded those who delight in and meditate on God's law (v. 2). Those who spend time taking in God's words will eventually yield a harvest.

When it comes to this psalm and its fruition, I find it fascinating to consider the thoughts of Patrick Henry Reardon in *Christ in the Psalms* (Conciliar Press, 2000). He says that because the language in the Hebrew is 'emphatically masculine', the man who is like a tree planted by the streams of water in verse 3 is Jesus. And thus, 'The Law of the Lord, which is to be our delight and meditation day and night, finds its meaning only in him' (p. 2).

As we chew over the words of scripture, asking God through his Spirit to sink them deeply into us, we will become more like Jesus. We too will be like a tree planted by a rich source of living water; we too will bear fruit in season. We may resist the labour needed in clearing the land and in planting and tending the seeds, but we can trust that God will multiply our efforts at the harvest.

Lord, give me the perseverance I need to bear crops that will please and honour you. Strengthen my feeble hands and help me not to lose heart. Amen
AMY BOUCHER PYE

A garden locked up

You are a garden locked up, my sister, my bride; you are a spring enclosed, a sealed fountain. Your plants are an orchard of pomegranates with choice fruits, with henna and nard, nard and saffron, calamus and cinnamon. (NIV)

In my 20s I blossomed in my relationship with God when I started to hear his still, small voice. As Oswald Chambers has said, when we hear God's voice, life becomes a romance. And life was a romance, but I also yearned for a lover with arms.

I prayed through many words of scripture, claiming them as my own, sensing God speaking them to me lovingly. And when I came to this passage in the Song of Songs, I pondered it deeply: 'You are a garden locked up, my sister, my bride; you are a spring enclosed, a sealed fountain' (v. 12). Interpreting it literally, I longed for the day when the garden would be unlocked by the man God would give me as my husband.

The Song of Songs celebrates the marital love between a husband and wife, and many theologians also see it as an allegory of the relationship between God and his beloved people. Whichever interpretation we are most comfortable with, we can ponder the picture of being a 'garden locked up… a spring enclosed, a sealed fountain'. Whether single or married, we can revel in being that sealed fountain or locked garden before God. He protects us and keeps us pure, forgiving us for whatever mistakes and errors we've committed. We can walk in the garden of our heart with him, knowing that he delights in us.

You can ask God to make your garden bloom; to refresh the waters in your spring. And he will answer, bringing forth life and love and peace. And the world will be changed by this intimate relationship between you and your God.

Loving God, you have made me for yourself, and my heart is restless until I find my rest in you. Seal my heart with your love, helping me to find the gift of true peace. Amen

AMY BOUCHER PYE

From a desert to a garden

'The Lord will surely comfort Zion and will look with compassion on all her ruins; he will make her deserts like Eden, her wastelands like the garden of the Lord.' (NIV)

Living after our first parents' disobedience, we can be weighed down by disease, disappointment, regret and weariness. When things don't go the way we hope, we have to reconcile our dreams with reality, which can feel shattering and hard.

Think of God's people in Isaiah's time. The prophet shared God's promises to the Israelites about how he would rescue them from exile after they'd been captured by the Babylonians. But as they hadn't yet been captured, they had to face the pain of this happening. Before they could enjoy God's rescue, first they'd be exiled from the promised land.

Knowing they'd lose heart, God called them to remember those who went before them – Abraham and Sarah, the couple who endured decades of infertility before becoming the parents of this new nation (v. 2). As the Israelites remembered God's deeds from years past, they'd more easily trust him to make good on his promises of comfort and compassion. And then God would 'make her deserts like Eden, her wastelands like the garden of the Lord. Joy and gladness will be found in her, thanksgiving and the sound of singing' (v. 3).

God promised that he'd turn the arid wasteland into the lush garden that Adam and Eve enjoyed before their disobedience. With this he said that not only would his people be released from the Babylonian captivity, but that one day they would enjoy a full return to his garden of paradise – a promise we'll return to when we look at the text of Revelation.

We're prone to lose heart, but we can look back at the many fulfilled promises of God as we seek to trust him more and more.

Loving Lord, when I feel like I'm bound in captivity, losing hope, remind me of how you've met me in so many ways in the past. Lift my gaze to you and help me to hope again. Amen

AMY BOUCHER PYE

A well-watered garden

'The Lord will guide you always; he will satisfy your needs in a sun-scorched land and will strengthen your frame. You will be like a well-watered garden, like a spring whose waters never fail.' (NIV)

God tired of his people's empty gestures. They fasted, but not whole-heartedly – on the days of the fast they still quarrelled and exploited their employees (vv. 3–4). What God wanted instead was a true fast, one to release the chains of exploitation and feed the hungry (vv. 6–7), one that his people approached with a full commitment.

And then God would bless them. He'd heal them and would be with them, answering them when they called (vv. 8–9). Note in verse 8 how God promised not only to go before them but also to follow them from behind, his glory their rear guard. God would guide them always, providing for them even in a 'sun-scorched land' where they would be 'like a well-watered garden, like a spring whose waters never fail' (v. 11).

I've never been to Israel, but I've led retreats in southern Spain, where I'm told the climate is similar to the Holy Land. I can relate to the weariness of the heat of the day in this sun-scorched land, my energy seeping out from the dry, hot conditions. God's promise of being made a well-watered garden with unfailing springs must have heartened his people, those who were accustomed to the sapping heat in an era of no air conditioning.

If you feel drained of energy when it comes to your walk with God, consider what might be behind that and how it could be restored. Perhaps, like God's people, you haven't been wholeheartedly committed to him. Know that as you place your trust in him, seeking to follow and honour him, he will restore and renew you. He'll provide for you the springs that will never fail.

Lord, when I fail you, help me to return to you. When I lack energy and commitment, strike my heart with love and devotion. Help me to serve you more. Amen

AMY BOUCHER PYE

Settling down

'Build houses and settle down; plant gardens and eat what they produce. Marry and have sons and daughters; find wives for your sons and give your daughters in marriage, so that they too may have sons and daughters.' (NIV)

When I was in the stage of yearning for a husband in my 20s, I landed on Jeremiah 29:6. I hoped and longed that God was highlighting it to me: 'Marry and have sons and daughters.' I was, of course, ignoring the original context, that of the Israelites being in captivity, away from the promised land. If God were indeed calling me to marry, would I be able to live my life away from my family and country of origin – as I now have for over two decades, having married my English husband? In my glee of thinking that this verse might come true for me, I didn't count the cost of what it would entail.

God was asking his people to trust him and to settle into life in captivity in Babylon. He would make them prosper there even as he did in Egypt. But they had to root themselves deeply into their situation, building houses and planting gardens. They were to pray even for the prosperity of their captors, for if the city to which they'd been exiled prospered, they too would prosper (v. 7).

I imagine it took God's people some internal wrangling before they consented to planting a garden while in captivity. As they longed to return home, they wouldn't have wanted to invest in where they were. But God was calling them to trust him even in that place, just as he welcomes us to look to him for comfort and direction when we feel homeless and adrift.

With God, consider if you face areas of resistance in your life. Are you withholding love or commitment in some way? How could God release you from a stiff-back stance?

Lord, make me pliable and responsive to your Spirit. Open my ears and my heart, that I might sense you moving in my life and respond with love and obedience. Amen

AMY BOUCHER PYE

Never again uprooted

'They will rebuild the ruined cities and live in them. They will plant vineyards and drink their wine; they will make gardens and eat their fruit. I will plant Israel in their own land, never again to be uprooted from the land I have given them.' (NIV)

It feels like we're cheating by skipping to the last bits of the prophecy of Amos. After all, the first nine-and-a-half chapters are filled with the words of God's judgement about exile and destruction. Amos' name even means 'burden' or 'burden bearer', which signifies the weight of the message he had to deliver. He didn't seek to be a prophet – he was a shepherd and farmer whom God called into service.

God's people had disappointed him greatly, but he didn't wash his hands of them. Instead he ended his message given through Amos with these words of hope and restoration. He invited them to look to him for the new wine that would flow from the mountains when he brought them back from exile (vv. 13–14). In the beautiful language of promise, he said he would 'plant Israel in their own land, never again to be uprooted' (v. 15). Israel as the vine would be placed deeply into the soil of home, to live there with God and to enjoy the fruit of the land.

This passage from Amos provides a wonderful link to the one we'll turn to tomorrow, where we hear that Jesus is the vine and God is the gardener. Jesus connects us to the Father while ushering in his kingdom through his acts of love and mercy. As we're joined to God through his Son and Spirit, we'll never be uprooted from our home with him.

You might want to read through verses 13 to 15 in the style of lectio divina, where you read the passage four times and ask God to highlight a word or phrase through the Spirit. As you do so, chew over the words and ask God to let them sink deeply into you.

Lord, establish my identity as your loved one. Help me to know that my home is in you, and there I belong. May this knowledge root me deeply in you and give me a deep and unshakeable foundation. Amen

AMY BOUCHER PYE

Our gardener

'I am the vine; you are the branches. If you remain in me and I in you, you will bear much fruit; apart from me you can do nothing.' (NIV)

Each year, in the fashion of #myoneword, I choose a word for the year along with a corresponding text from scripture. For 2021, my word was 'abide' and the passage was this one from John 15. I've long loved this talk that Jesus had with his friends after they'd eaten their last supper together and as they walked to the garden of Gethsemane.

Jesus tells of his Father being the gardener, and how he 'cuts off every branch in me that bears no fruit, while every branch that does bear fruit he prunes so that it will be even more fruitful' (v. 2). Abiding gives us the strength to bear the pruning, to which our gardener subjects each of us so that we'll bear more fruit for him. It's painful, but we trust that God wields the secateurs with love and care, for he knows how the pruning will help us to grow stronger and to be more rooted in him.

For me, abiding in 2021 looked like clinging closely to Jesus day by day, seeking his nourishment through the Spirit so that I could love and refresh others. As I remained with him moment by moment during the challenges I faced, I received an infilling of his strength, love and presence. The pruning felt excruciating at times, but I never doubted God's love for me.

Can you look back at seasons of pruning in your own life and trace how God shaped you through those times? If so, ponder how God's faithfulness in the past can help you as you face the challenges of the moment. And know that with him, you'll bear fruit that will last (v. 16).

Lord Jesus, help me to remain with you. May the sap of the Spirit flow through me, uniting me to the Father through you. Help me to obey your commands and remain in your love. Amen

AMY BOUCHER PYE

Squeezed

Then Jesus went with his disciples to a place called Gethsemane, and he said to them, 'Sit here while I go over there and pray.' He took Peter and the two sons of Zebedee along with him, and he began to be sorrowful and troubled. (NIV)

My friends in Spain have several olive trees on the land of their retreat centre, and in the autumn they harvest the olives one by one. Packing their van full of huge buckets of their pickings, they take what they've gathered to a large centre for processing. Massive machines squeeze every last drop of oil out of the olives in this first pressing; in return my friends take home jugs of extra virgin olive oil – the purest and best – to use in the coming year.

The garden where Jesus prayed on the night he was betrayed is called Gethsemane, which means oil press. The garden was probably an olive-tree orchard, with Jesus and his friends lent its use by the landowner. As he withdrew to pray, he invited his inner-circle disciples to support him as he faced the horrendous task he'd soon undergo, dying on the cross.

The name Gethsemane is apt because Jesus was squeezed in anguish even to the point that his sweat was like drops of blood, as we see in Luke's gospel (Luke 22:44). He asked three times for his Father to take the cup of suffering from him, but he aligned his will with the Father's and accepted the task before him.

And the disciples? They couldn't stay awake while Jesus poured out his heart and soul to the Father. Their eyes heavy, they kept falling back to sleep, even though Jesus roused them. When I think that I'd do better, I remember the many times I've let Jesus down and understand that I too would fall asleep. But Jesus knows our frailty and never stops loving us. As we remember how he spent himself on our behalf, we can grow ever more thankful.

Loving Jesus, you prayed in anguish at the thought of the cross, and yet you obeyed the will of the Father. Help me to face the hard things before me and stay obedient to you. Amen

AMY BOUCHER PYE

The garden tomb

At the place where Jesus was crucified, there was a garden, and in the garden a new tomb, in which no one had ever been laid. (NIV)

As we've seen, life began in a garden. Adam and Eve walked with God, naked and unafraid before they disobeyed their creator. Because of their actions – and those of their children and children's children – Jesus had to die and be buried in a tomb. This too was in a garden, where life began in a whole new way.

Mary had gone to the garden tomb to mourn the death of Jesus, but when she got there, she found the stone had moved and his body was no longer there. She ran to tell Peter and John, and after they came and saw they returned to the other disciples. Only Mary remained at the tomb, weeping and mourning, when Jesus appeared to her. Notice Jesus' great love in revealing himself to a woman who loved him; he could have appeared to John and Peter along with her moments before. But he saved his appearance just for her – a gift of tenderness and love.

Notice too how she realised who he was only when he spoke her name. As with Mary, we come to our deepest sense of identity when we respond to the voice of Jesus, calling our name. We know we are his beloved.

If you have time today, why not read through this story and ask God to help you imagine yourself as a character in it? You might be Mary, Peter or John, or you might be an unseen bystander, observing the story unfold. Ask God through his Spirit to reveal himself to you in a deep way through your imagination. Often we can get in touch with our emotions, sometimes those that have been buried, through this mode of prayer.

Risen Christ, you call me by name; you know me. Help me to see myself as you see me. Help me to live out of this deepest sense of knowing and being known. Amen

AMY BOUCHER PYE

A new heaven and a new earth

Then I saw 'a new heaven and a new earth,' for the first heaven and the first earth had passed away, and there was no longer any sea. (NIV)

When Jesus revealed to the aging disciple John a vision of things to come, he showed him 'a new heaven and a new earth' – the new Jerusalem, the Holy City (vv. 1–2). This will fulfil the prophecy given to Isaiah, when God said: 'See, I will create new heavens and a new earth. The former things will not be remembered, nor will they come to mind' (Isaiah 65:17). In that prophecy, God promised that his people would live in this new land where they would 'build houses and dwell in them'; they would 'plant vineyards and eat their fruit' (Isaiah 65:21). And no longer would they plant what others would eat (Isaiah 65:22).

We don't know exactly how the prophecy to Isaiah and the revelation to John have been and will be fulfilled. That is, how much of Isaiah's prophecy was fulfilled to God's people before the coming of Jesus, after they left captivity? Or does the promise of building homes and planting vineyards and gardens in the new heaven and earth mean that we will do some form of work in heaven? We just don't know, but it's a joyous thing to contemplate work as God intended it – labouring without toil; applying our unique creativity and gifts to bringing forth life; having our own patch of garden where no weeds will burst through and no pests will render our fruit spoiled.

In the meantime, we partner with God as he brings forth his kingdom here and now. In faith we plant the seeds from which will come sunflowers and tomatoes and herbs. In faith we bring up our children in the knowledge of the love of God. And in faith we share the truth of God's love, and we fight injustice and promote goodness and beauty.

Rescuing Lord, you usher in a new heaven and a new earth, where we dwell with you. Help me to partner with you in this new venture of life and love. Amen

AMY BOUCHER PYE

A garden oasis

Then the angel showed me the river of the water of life, as clear as crystal, flowing from the throne of God and of the Lamb down the middle of the great street of the city. On each side of the river stood the tree of life. (NIV)

We have come full circle – life in paradise will involve a city that has a garden at its heart. In this final book in the Bible, we glimpse the amazing picture of God and Jesus at the centre on the throne and flowing from them the river of life that brings growth and healing (v. 1). On each side of the river, similar to what we saw in Psalm 1, stands the tree of life. Imagine a tree that can bear twelve crops of fruit, one each month! It's a mind-bending image of bounty and goodness.

A friend shared how when his mother was near to death, he read to her these last chapters of Revelation. Sitting next to her bed in the hospital where she would soon take her last breath, he welcomed her to fill her mind with images of the life she would soon be entering. As he read, he could see God's peace settle in deeply around her, her nervous fears abating. When he spoke of God's people seeing his face, hers shone with joy and radiance. Although he was achingly sad when she died, he felt comforted to know that he'd shared her last moments pondering the glories to come.

We don't need to wait to consider this revelation of the glories that await us. It's a good practice to read through these last couple of chapters as we ask God to spark in us hope for things to come. You might want to interact with the images through painting or sketching a picture, or writing a poem, or planting some flowers in the garden.

Know that God welcomes you to reside in the garden, to find rest and love in his presence. I hope to see you there!

Father, Son and Holy Spirit, thank you for your kingdom of life and grace, not only in the age to come but also for how you're bringing it forth now. I worship and thank you for your goodness and love. Amen

AMY BOUCHER PYE

What the Bible teaches about age

Selina Stone writes:

When we take a look through the scriptures, we get the impression that for God, age is very much just a number. In all senses, God's perspective on age stands against that of contemporary society. While our world today values the potential of youth, in the scriptures we find countless stories of extraordinary events and moments taking place in the lives of those who are middle-aged and elderly. In God's economy, anything is possible!

We also find that, though society tends not to take young people seriously because of their lack of experience, God calls children and young people at a time when adults may consider them to be not the right candidates. God gives purpose to any person God chooses, at any stage of life.

This is a great encouragement to us as we journey through life and face the temptation to imagine that our best days are behind us or to be anxious about the future. Our lives do not have to be limited by the social or cultural expectations of what should happen at particular times in our lives, even when we have adopted those same expectations. As in the cases of Sarah, Anna and Caleb, God is able to bring to fruition those things we hope and pray for, even if it takes longer than we might have expected.

While we can often focus inwardly on our own lives and the passing of time, God sees our lives as part of a much bigger story which is not just about us. Our lives are found in God, who at every stage and age is seeking to bring about fullness of life within us, that will be a light in the midst of creation. Whether we are a newborn baby, a young child, a young adult or someone more mature in age, our days are held within the hand of God who delights in us. Therefore, we can be sure that there are wonderful surprises to be discovered as God, who is already present in our coming ages, awaits us.

My prayer is that these reflections will inspire you to grow in peace as you remember that your time belongs to God, and that they will encourage you to hope in what God might bring about in your life in the years to come.

Loved through the ages

My frame was not hidden from you when I was made in the secret place, when I was woven together in the depths of the earth. Your eyes saw my unformed body; all the days ordained for me were written in your book before one of them came to be. (NIV)

This is one of the most well-known psalms, popular no doubt because of the overall reminder that we are not alone. While we might be tempted to imagine that we are simply passing through the universe relatively unknown or known solely by the people close to us, we are reminded here of God's eternal love and knowledge of each one of us. The psalmist imagines being in the 'secret place' and having an 'unformed body' and says (in my own translation) 'even when no one else could see me, and I was still becoming myself, God's eyes were on me'.

Being seen by God throughout the length of our days can only be a comfort when we know *how* God looks upon us. In our lifetimes people can look at us with very different eyes: some view us with hope, others with envy; some look upon us with kindness, others with disapproval. When we consider the gaze of God upon us, this psalm gives us a picture of a God who cares enough to be close to us even when we are hidden and no one else is there. The gaze of God is the gaze of one who loves us enough to name every day of our lives even before we begin to live them.

As we begin these reflections on age, we must start from the basic thought that God is not only present with us now, but also has been and will be present with us through all of our ages. While elements of our past may be a blur, our present may be complex and our future unclear, for God there is no mystery to our story. God knows it all.

As you take time to pray today, begin by imagining yourself being gazed upon by God with great delight. What would you like to bring to God as you consider that God knows all the days ordained for you?

SELINA STONE

Defending the young and vulnerable

The midwives… feared God and did not do what the king of Egypt had told them to do [kill the baby boys born to Hebrew women]; they let the boys live… So God was kind to the midwives and the people increased and became even more numerous. (NIV)

It is probably difficult for us to imagine such a political context where a king would write infanticide into law. Pharaoh (like many before and after him) is the kind of leader who will do anything to maintain his own power and the dominance of people who are just like him. These babies, who would already have been vulnerable in any normal context, are born into violent circumstances, which some of them undoubtedly did not survive. Their first breath and last breath are much closer than any of us would hope for any child.

For children around the world, life is filled with the threat of violence, if not at the hands of an individual, then due to systems of poverty and inequality. Children suffer today due to domestic violence and abuses of many kinds. Almost 7.5 million children and young people died of preventable diseases around the world in 2019. Here in the UK, child hunger and homelessness are ever increasing as socio-economic inequality grows more severe. The lives of our children continue to be under threat.

Yet the hopeful aspect of this story is found in the midwives who resist what has come to be accepted in Egypt: they will not kill the baby boys, as others presumably are. These women risk their lives by defying the unjust order in order to preserve the lives of these young babies. We are not told whether Moses was one of the babies who was saved by these particular midwives, but someone must have followed their example and saved the boy who would grow up to save the nation. These midwives were not in traditional positions of power but used what they had to defend those who could not defend themselves.

As you consider this story, are there particular children or vulnerable groups you would like to pray for? In your own context, how might the midwives inspire you to act with or for those who are desperately in need?

SELINA STONE

God's call to the young

The boy Samuel ministered before the Lord under Eli. In those days the word of the Lord was rare; there were not many visions. One night… the lamp of God had not yet gone out, and Samuel was lying down in the house of the Lord… Then the Lord called Samuel. (NIV)

As someone who grew up going to church and learned to hear God from a young age, Samuel's story helps me to make sense of my own faith journey. But as an adult reading about Samuel, I feel the burden of his particular journey. He is a miracle baby, born after the many prayers of his mother Hannah, who makes a vow to God that if she gets pregnant, she will give the child into God's service.

Hannah does get pregnant and so Samuel is sent away from his mother, father and siblings as soon as he is weaned, to live with Eli and his sons. Hannah has more children after him and so his family seem to move on without him. This must have been a tough journey for Samuel. Yet in this moment, on a normal night in the temple, something extraordinary happens: the Lord calls him by name.

Samuel's story reminds us that God looks for the qualities which we often overlook. Samuel is young and relatively inexperienced as far as ministry goes; he does not realise that it is God who is calling him at first! Eli helps Samuel by affirming that it might be God calling him, even though it might seem unlikely at a time when the word of the Lord was rare. God breaks the silence in order to speak to this young boy.

What was God waiting for? Maybe for someone with an open heart rather than a fixed agenda to sit and be still long enough for God to speak. I am not convinced that God has favourites but rather that God desires to be with each of us and to speak with each of us. We are all welcome regardless of our age, if only we find the time.

As you sit in God's presence like Samuel, what would you like to say to God? What might God say to you in reply? Who might you call on to help you discern the voice of God in your own life?

SELINA STONE

God who equips the young

'Alas, Sovereign Lord,' [Jeremiah] said, 'I do not know how to speak; I am too young.' But the Lord said to me, 'Do not say, "I am too young." You must go to everyone I send you to and say whatever I command you. Do not be afraid of them.' (NIV)

One of the great joys of being young is having the freedom to admit that you do not know, without any shame. As adults we often do not know, but we feel that we should. It can be difficult to admit to ourselves, to others and even to God that we are unsure or have no idea at all.

Jeremiah shows us what honesty looks like: as soon as God calls him, he is honest about his limitations, knowing that there is no shame in telling God the truth he feels. Notice that God doesn't say, 'Yes, you do know how to speak'; Jeremiah was correct about his lack of experience. Yet God assures him that he will make up the gap. Where Jeremiah's self-perception is incorrect is in his statement that he is 'too young'. God does not answer that particular fear; he simply persists in telling him what he needs to do, thus undermining any notion that Jeremiah's age is a problem for God's purpose.

If humility could be defined as having a right perspective on yourself in relation to God and others, then Jeremiah is not humble but insecure; he thinks too little of himself. Insecurity can masquerade as humility in our own lives very easily – do we not take that role because we are humble or because we are afraid that we are too… (I'll let you fill in the blank)? In this passage we are reminded that it is God who has the final word in how we should see ourselves and what we might do with God's help. When God calls us to opportunities that feel intimidating, the humble response is to say 'yes'. Even though we might feel inadequate, the God who calls will give us what we need.

Lord, it is easy for me to feel afraid or uncertain about what lies ahead. Give me the strength of your Holy Spirit that I might say 'yes' to your call, and to all those opportunities to be obedient to your guidance in all areas of life. Amen
SELINA STONE

The power of a young woman

Now bands of raiders from Aram had gone out and had taken captive a young girl from Israel, and she served Naaman's wife. She said to her mistress, 'If only my master would see the prophet who is in Samaria! He would cure him of his leprosy.' (NIV)

We are not often encouraged to listen to the advice of children. Adults who have power listen to other adults who have power, not often to children or young people, who are powerless in their eyes. Yet in this intriguing story Naaman, a military general for the nation of Aram, is healed through the advice of a young slave girl.

Young girls are almost totally absent in biblical stories except as victims of violence, so this story shines brightly. This unnamed young girl is living in captivity because of a war against her people, but she exercises her agency and her voice to impact a situation through compassion. Her role is not acknowledged by Naaman, who is healed because of her, and we do not know whether she is freed, which is itself an injustice. However, this young girl is surely an example for us all.

It is not uncommon for young girls, who are vulnerable in so many ways, to find themselves in positions of oppression and living under forms of captivity. The Bible draws our attention to their plight, through this story. Around the world young women live in slavery far away from family and safety, including in the UK. Many young women who appear to be free live captive to poverty or to oppressions in the mind and emotions. When we hear about the plight of young women like this, we might be horrified or moved to tears. But what does it mean for those of us who have the freedom to use our agency on their behalf? How might we receive the love of God in our own hearts, and stand in solidarity with our sisters who suffer?

As you pray today, bring to God all of those young women who live in danger and captivity, those who are tormented and distressed. How might God be making you more aware of the young women around you?

SELINA STONE

The freedom of youth

After three days they found him in the temple courts, sitting among the teachers, listening to them and asking them questions… His mother said to him, 'Son, why have you treated us like this?'… He asked, 'Didn't you know I had to be in my Father's house?' (NIV)

If ever there was a passage that captured the strain that occurs when a child begins to find their own agency beyond the will of their parents, then this is it! Jesus, who is like us in all ways except sin, exhibits what many parents might consider to be atrocious behaviour – and even (dare I say it?) a bit of an attitude. Jesus has left his parents without their permission and gone back to the major city of Jerusalem to sit among the teachers of the law, while his parents continue to travel home. Any adult who has temporarily lost a child in a supermarket will empathise with Mary's question, which I am quite sure was accompanied with a look of relief mixed with anger. Jesus seems oblivious to their concerns, saying (paraphrased), 'Chill out, Mum. Obviously, I'd be here in the temple!'

Jesus models the normal and necessary stage of life where a young person begins to explore what it is they want and need to flourish. Jesus is totally human; he must learn and develop like any other twelve-year-old, and even he has a need to develop that clashes with how his parents think he should behave. Jesus is more aware than his parents of what he needs and what his journey will involve. The need to move past people-pleasing is true for all of us, whatever age we are. We are all growing and changing. Jesus helps us to see that it is not sinful to disappoint others, nor is it a sin to put yourself in the position to get what you need for your journey. It is in fact a holy and divine act to learn, grow and flourish as God designed.

Visualise yourself in this story: are you travelling with Mary and Joseph to meet their expectations? Or are you able to free yourself to grow into the person you feel called to be? Bring this to God in prayer.

SELINA STONE

Warnings to the young

This sin of the young men was very great in the Lord's sight, for they were treating the Lord's offering with contempt... Now Eli, who was very old, heard about everything his sons were doing to all Israel... So he said to them, 'Why do you do such things?' (NIV)

Though being young comes with great opportunities for learning and growth, it also involves many temptations. If Samuel, Jeremiah, the young girl and the young Jesus exemplify the former, then Eli's sons exhibit the latter. They are disrespectful to the community and dishonouring to God. They have a father who questions their behaviour, but they do not listen. They not only fail to do what is right, but they also fail to consider the consequences of their behaviour. They are doomed to repeat their evil behaviour and to suffer the consequences of their wayward path.

Some of us may have been like Eli's sons: arrogant and determined to get our own way no matter the consequences. We may have disrespected boundaries and rules in ways which did harm to other people. On the other hand, we may have been victimised by such people who were bullies or abusers. I definitely had my own experiences of such people as a young woman. It is easy for us to blame the individual for what they have become, but the more complex question is to ask what contributed to them becoming like this.

Eli's sons meet a brutal end alongside their father, as God holds Eli responsible for not doing enough to correct them. This is not a suggestion that parents are always to blame, but rather that children and young people reflect back to us the society and communities which we adults have created. What are we teaching young people to value, through what they see us value? How are we teaching young people what it means to be humans made in the image of God? What are we modelling which shows young people what it means to be disciples of Jesus? It surely takes a whole village to raise a child.

As you pray today, reflect on your own youth as you consider those young people who seem wayward in your community and the nation. Pray for them as you pray for yourself, that we might create a better world.

SELINA STONE

Age and beauty

The glory of young [people] is their strength, grey hair the splendour of the old. (NIV)

In our culture, age and beauty are often opposed to one another. The common adage 'age before beauty' is used to encourage younger women (who are supposed to embody 'beauty') to respect and defer to older women (who represent 'age'). Yet in this short verse, the scriptures indicate that there is no need to choose between the two! On the contrary, splendour (which is so much more than beauty) comes with age, and specifically with the grey hair that we are often so keen to get rid of.

I have had a few grey hairs since my late 20s, so I am gaining my splendour early! But overall we struggle with the signs of ageing, whether grey hairs, wrinkles or sagging skin. We buy products that promise to keep us looking young so that we might hold on to the glory of youth. But slowing time is impossible (just watch *Death Becomes Her* if you want proof), and in the light of this scripture we might ask ourselves whether it is even desirable. Do we risk neglecting the splendour of the various ages that lie ahead of us?

Ageing is one of the most humbling aspects of human existence. This is a process we cannot control or manage no matter how much we might want to. But this verse encourages us to look at our own lives with hope – not that we can stay young forever, but that as we change, we are gaining a splendour that we did not have when we were younger. This splendour is more than skin-deep; it is cultivated through experience and wisdom, and the grace and mercy that follow us along the way.

Dear God, we recognise that we do not control time but that you hold time in your hands. Help us to remain humble, trusting you with the days ahead of us as you move us from glory to splendour. Amen

SELINA STONE

Loving formation for older people

Do not rebuke an older man harshly, but exhort him as if he were your father. Treat younger men as brothers, older women as mothers, and younger women as sisters, with absolute purity. (NIV)

Intergenerational communities can be a joy and a challenge, and here we find guidelines for how they might be done well. It begins with advice on how to speak to older men who need to be corrected – an interesting place to start. We can imagine that older people are automatically wise and know how to behave appropriately, but of course in reality older people can simply be deeply set in their harmful or foolish ways. This passage brings this to our attention; it is not only young people who need to be corrected at times. When that is needed, the writer suggests that it should be done with respect, as you would speak to your father. By extension, everyone should be treated as if they are family within the church.

In family and church life, the task of developing good relationships can be difficult. It requires honesty and sensitivity, love and truth, kindness and challenge. When it comes to speaking to older people, this can be even more difficult. In certain cultures, it is taught that older people must always be obeyed and never questioned, as a mark of respect. In our Christian communities, the command to 'honour your father and mother' can lead to a reluctance to set boundaries or to speak up when something a parent does is wrong or unjust. But this scripture indicates to us that loving older people involves challenging unhealthy or harmful behaviour. How can we help them to love and to grow in character and discipleship if we simply allow them to repeat what is harmful to themselves or others? It is natural to want to avoid this, but we are encouraged to 'exhort' (earnestly advise) older people with love and kindness, as we would our own family.

As you pray today, consider your parents, mentors or parent figures in your own life. Is there an unresolved issue you would like to pray about today? Is there some action that God might lead you to take?

SELINA STONE

Older dreamers

'And afterwards, I will pour out my Spirit on all people. Your sons and daughters will prophesy, your old [people] will dream dreams, your young [people] will see visions.' (NIV)

As we have seen, God often chooses unexpected people to be at the centre of his plans. So far, we have considered one group of those unexpected – the young and inexperienced. However, it is also true that older people can be considered to be redundant within the work of God in the world. Though we think of retirement from work as the norm for older people, we can sometimes act as if there is a spiritual equivalent! In church life we can stop calling on older people, despite the fact that they have some of the most wonderful gifts to offer the community to complement the energetic input of younger people. In this verse in Joel, we see very clearly that God does not in fact have a retirement plan in mind for older people: when the Spirit is poured out on all people, old people will dream dreams, while young people see visions.

To speak of dreaming dreams is not to suggest that old people will enjoy afternoon naps when the Spirit is poured out (lovely as afternoon naps are, even for someone in their 30s). Rather, it is to say that older people will have the capacity to imagine what should be. Dreams appear in many places in the scriptures, being moments when God speaks to people directly. For Jacob, Joseph (Jacob's son) and Joseph (Mary's husband), God shared great mysteries and directed their paths through dreams. Of course, young people dream too, and older people do have visions, but the wonderful point of this passage is that God does not leave older people out of the promise. The revelations older people receive from God, as well as their wider gifts and their voices, matter in God's mind, for the community of believers and for the future of the world.

Pray for the older people in your family, church and community, that they might experience the fullness of the Holy Spirit in their lives and dream the dreams that God might give them.

SELINA STONE

An elderly trailblazer

There was also a prophet, Anna, the daughter of Penuel... She was very old; she had lived with her husband seven years after her marriage, and then was a widow until she was eighty-four. She never left the temple but worshipped night and day, fasting and praying. (NIV)

Christian history is filled with stories of women like Anna. Many of these women are unknown faithful lovers of God who have served churches and communities in the name of Christ. Some of them have made personal sacrifices that only they and God will ever know, and they have never been recognised for it. They are the women who pray consistently when others are busy or distracted, and they maintain the spiritual wells of Christian communities around the world. They are friends of God who know God's voice and are happy to wait for God's promises.

Anna can feel a long way away from where we are – if not in terms of age, then maybe in terms of circumstance. Maybe we struggle to commit to rhythms of prayer and worship, let alone being like Anna, who worships day and night and never leaves the temple! But Anna is an example of an older woman who takes a special path which can inspire us.

Anna has suffered loss in her life and yet she finds a place of fulfilment despite the grief she has endured for many years. She commits her life to God and resists social expectations to marry again. Anna blazes her own trail as an older single woman and, in the end, she has the privilege of a particular encounter with God as she sees the baby Jesus. Despite all of the twists and turns of her long journey, she finds herself at 84 in the right place at the right time. She set her life to the pace of God, not her own or that of the people around her, and gained her reward.

To God, who brings beauty out of ashes in our lives and the world: as you did for Anna, guide me along the path of life, which twists and turns, to places of flourishing and encounter with you. Amen

SELINA STONE

The God who defies nature

Sarah laughed to herself… 'After I am worn out and my [husband] is old, will I now have this pleasure?' Then the Lord said to Abraham, 'Why did Sarah laugh and say, "Will I really have a child, now that I am old?" Is anything too hard for the Lord?' (NIV)

Most of us who pray have wondered whether what we are praying and hoping for is ever going to happen. Yet we mostly hope for things which seem perfectly reasonable rather than praying for the impossible (even though it might feel like it). But Sarah has been told to hope and wait for what is naturally impossible. She went through the menopause years ago, she is physically weaker (the Bible says she is not just old, but *very* old), and she and Abraham are probably not even having sex anymore! But now she is being told that she will get pregnant and give birth to a baby. When she laughs – which is a perfectly reasonable response to what I have just outlined – she is told (my paraphrase), 'God can do this, just you wait!'

This story does more than encourage us to believe that God can enable an elderly couple to have a baby; it inspires us to believe that what we might consider impossible (not just unlikely) is not a barrier to what God might do in and through our lives. This story acts as a symbol for us to look at every time we are tempted to believe that something we have longed for for a very long time can never happen. When the deadlines we set are passed time and time again, until we give up and laugh at the idea that it could happen, it is still not too late for the promise to come to pass. Hope can be painful when it seems only to be met with disappointment. I imagine Sarah had given up hope, but God had not given up on the promise even when she did. So we can be honest. God is faithful even when we struggle.

As you reflect on your own life, is there an area where you are asking for what seems impossible or very unlikely? Do you need the courage to hope and to pray again? Bring this to God in prayer.

SELINA STONE

Taking ground

'So here I [Caleb] am today, eighty-five years old! I am still as strong today as the day Moses sent me out; I'm just as vigorous to go out to battle now as I was then. Now give me this hill country that the Lord promised me that day.' (NIV)

If Sarah represents the feeling of hopelessness that can come from enduring many disappointments over a long time and not being able to do anything about it, then Caleb represents the bold determination that people can exhibit when they have some sense of agency over their circumstances. Caleb, unlike Sarah, can do something to get what he has been promised, and he is not shy about using whatever means are at his disposal. He makes his case to Joshua by drawing on the people's history, quoting Moses and affirming that he has the capacity to do what it takes to take the land that was promised to him. He recognises that this is not just a fight for himself, but in order that he might have an inheritance for all those who would come after him.

Whether or not we have children, Caleb inspires us to recognise our place within the story of our community and humanity as a whole. Rather than resting on his laurels and enjoying his years, he understands that he has a responsibility to prepare the way for the new generation. In our own culture, which is so focused on the nuclear family, this can easily be misunderstood to encourage us to selfish greed for our own children's sake. But as people called to love not just our own children but all of humanity, our responsibilities extend beyond this. Caleb secures land in this passage, and yet we are complicit in the destruction of land through the environmental crisis of our time. As an older person he sets an example for all of us, at whatever stage of life, to be mindful of what we are fighting for and what we are leaving behind.

As you reflect on this passage today, consider what environment you are leaving behind for the generations to come. What action might you take to help to secure the land for our human family?

SELINA STONE

Recognising our agelessness

Abraham lived a hundred and seventy-five years. Then Abraham breathed his last and died at a good old age, an old man and full of years; and he was gathered to his people. (NIV)

In this last reflection on age, we find ourselves coming full circle. We started in eternity, recognising God as one who knows each of our ordained days before we have lived one of them. We end with this wonderful image of Abraham being gathered into an eternal community of those who have gone on before him. This passage reminds us that, while we might have various concerns about age, there is a core element of each of us that is ageless. We are not simply bodies getting older, but spiritual beings eternally held by God within a wider body of God's children through time and space. Our individualistic culture can cause us to forget this, but the Jewish tradition, alongside many other cultures, remembers our shared history, our connection to our ancestors and our collective futures. Abraham, like us, was not only moving towards a point of departure from the community he knew on earth, but was also approaching a point of arrival into a community which is beyond the material world.

Keeping sight of the eternal helps us to hold all of the complexity of our relatively short earthly lives in perspective. Abraham dies at a 'good age' not only because he is old, but also because he walked with God and lived the life he was called to. My mum was gathered to her people at 54, which was too soon for us, but her life was rich and wonderful, and she left us many gifts. However long we have we cannot know, and hopefully we will live to a 'good old age' like Abraham. But if life is shorter, it can still be a good life. Our lives go on beyond these days, and whether we are here or in eternity, they are held in the hands of our loving God.

Offer a prayer of thanks for family members and ancestors who have passed on ahead of you and remember the gifts they have left behind. What kind of legacy would you hope to leave? Offer this to God in prayer.

SELINA STONE

Ezra: a tale of revival and rebuilding

Caroline Fletcher writes:

The book of Ezra covers a period of around 80 years. It begins in the sixth century, 70 years into the Jewish exile in Babylon. Many Jews had been forcibly taken from their native land to this foreign city after the Babylonian army had conquered their country in 587BC, destroying Jerusalem and its magnificent temple. This was a devastating event for the Jews, and their prophets believed it was punishment for their unfaithfulness to the Lord in creating idols and worshipping foreign gods. The book of Ezra, however, marks a turning point in their fortunes, for it begins with Cyrus, the king of Persia, giving them permission to return to their native land and to rebuild Jerusalem and its temple.

This challenge was not easy, though: their country was lying in ruins. The book of Ezra makes it clear that even though their mission was inspired, initiated and enabled by God, it was still beset with problems. The returning exiles faced opposition from the surrounding peoples who stirred up trouble. These people even managed to halt the project for a time, causing the Jews to become discouraged and grow weary of the task.

Even when the temple was finally complete, the Jews were still struggling. They were tempted to drift back into their old idolatrous habits through the influence of the non-Jews around them. Despite their good intentions, they did not find doing God's will easy, something we can all relate to.

The book of Ezra may be set in a time very different to our own, one that seems alien to us, but the challenges those Jews faced are similar to the ones we experience when we seek to obey God: the weaknesses of our own human nature and the temptations and challenges of living in a society that does not share our faith.

Despite these problems, the book of Ezra is full of hope. It describes a group of people managing to serve God through the difficulties and succeeding in the task God had given them when the odds were stacked against them. It encourages us that with the help and guidance of a merciful God, fallible people can achieve great things, for these ordinary human beings rebuilt their city from the ashes and revived their nation's ailing faith.

God is faithful

In the first year of Cyrus king of Persia, in order to fulfil the word of the Lord spoken by Jeremiah, the Lord moved the heart of Cyrus king of Persia to make a proclamation throughout his realm and also to put it in writing. (NIV)

If you are puzzled about exactly what is going on in today's reading, that's hardly surprising! A lot of prior information is assumed: it can feel a bit like reading a sequel without having looked at the first volume. To understand this chapter, we need to go back 70 years from when Ezra starts to a terrible event in Jewish history: the destruction of Jerusalem and its magnificent temple by the Babylonians. Many Jews were taken captive and forced into exile in Babylon, which raised questions about their relationship with God. The promised land God had led them out of Egypt to possess was now no longer theirs. Did this mean God had rejected them? After all, prophets like Jeremiah had told them the exile was punishment for worshipping idols.

When we go through dark times, we often find ourselves asking similar questions. We can be tempted to wonder if God has forgotten about us or does not care about what we are going through. However, our reading from Ezra reassures us that God never gives up on his people. Even though the people of Israel had let him down, God restored them to the promised land, bringing their exile to an end just as Jeremiah had predicted (Jeremiah 29:10). And God used an unlikely person to achieve this: Cyrus, the king of Persia. Cyrus had defeated the Babylonians and taken over their empire. Now 70 years after Jerusalem's destruction, he decreed God's people could finally return home.

We often do not understand why God allows us to suffer. However, the message of Ezra is that God's love is unbreakable. Difficult times never mean God has given up on us. Ezra encourages us that we can trust God, no matter how bleak things may seem, for he is always faithful.

If you are suffering in any way, be honest with God about your feelings and ask him to give you a renewed sense of his love.

CAROLINE FLETCHER

Getting our priorities right

On the first day of the seventh month they began to offer burnt offerings to the Lord, though the foundation of the Lord's temple had not yet been laid. (NIV)

Thousands of Israelites acted upon King Cyrus' edict and returned to Jerusalem. However, others chose to stay in Babylon, for most had been born and raised there. Those that undertook the arduous 900-mile journey must have been extremely committed to rebuilding Jerusalem and its temple. So, it is surprising that the first thing these returnees did was not rebuild the temple, as Cyrus' edict allowed. Instead, they set up an altar and re-established daily sacrifices. This is particularly surprising because the temple had been central to their faith: they believed God dwelt there. Surely rebuilding it as quickly as possible would have boosted morale, stirred up their faith and provided a comfortable place to worship out of the elements?

But these returnees had learned a thing or two during their 70 years of exile. They re-established the sacrificial system first because they wanted to make a fresh start. Offering daily sacrifices was a way of acknowledging the seriousness of their sin and saying sorry for the wrong they had done. The Israelites wanted to walk closely with God in this new chapter of their history and avoid the mistakes that had led to their exile.

We no longer sacrifice animals as they did, but we can still learn from what motivated the ritual. Repentance was important to them but is something often neglected today: it can seem depressing to think about mistakes we have made. However, the point of repentance is not to weigh us down with guilt and make us feel bad. Recognising how far we fall short encourages us to seek God's help to change, for we realise we can't by ourselves. It also encourages us not to take forgiveness for granted and helps us appreciate God's mercy more. Do we take time to say sorry?

Spend time bringing to God things that you have done wrong and say sorry for those things. Ask for his help to change and thank him for his mercy and forgiveness.

CAROLINE FLETCHER

Keeping faith

They went immediately to the Jews in Jerusalem and compelled them by force to stop. Thus the work on the house of God in Jerusalem came to a standstill until the second year of the reign of Darius king of Persia. (NIV)

The returnees were busy rebuilding the temple, and we might assume this would be straightforward because they were doing God's will. However, our chapter shows that they faced a huge amount of opposition. Tensions began when people from the surrounding areas offered to help rebuild the temple. This might sound positive, but the passage calls them enemies. 2 Kings 17:33 gives us some background which explains why: these people worshipped pagan gods as well as the Lord. Their plan for the temple, then, probably involved turning it into a shrine where idols would be worshipped.

When the Jews refused these people's help, their opposition grew. They actively discouraged and intimidated the Jews, bribing officials to make false reports about them to their Persian rulers. We are given the text of a slanderous letter they sent, claiming the Jews were disloyal subjects who would not pay their taxes. And, sadly, their scheming worked: the Jews were ordered not to continue the rebuilding which held the project up for years.

How did these Jews feel? They had worked so hard, only for things to grind to a halt. Where was the Almighty in all this, and how could humans spoil his plans? Have you ever been surprised to encounter opposition and difficulty when you've been trying to serve God? This passage is a reminder that in this fallen world such things happen. But we can take encouragement from the wider perspective of the book of Ezra, for its writer knew that the temple and city would be rebuilt and that this delay was only temporary. This reminds us, then, not to lose sight of the bigger picture when we face difficulties and to hold on to hope, for although things may seem dark for a time, God's purposes cannot be held back forever.

Have you ever experienced difficulties or opposition when trying to serve God? How well did you cope with these problems and how did they affect your faith?

CAROLINE FLETCHER

God speaks

Now Haggai the prophet and Zechariah the prophet… prophesied to the Jews in Judah and Jerusalem in the name of the God of Israel, who was over them. Then Zerubbabel son of Shealtiel and Joshua son of Jozadak set to work to rebuild the house of God in Jerusalem. (NIV)

Around 15 years have gone by since Cyrus' edict which allowed the Jews to rebuild the temple, yet still it lay in ruins. They had grown weary and lost heart after all the opposition they had faced. However, things changed when two prophets, Haggai and Zechariah, appeared on the scene, proclaiming that the time had come to start rebuilding the temple again. Their prophecies can be read in the Old Testament books which bear their names. And the rebuilding did seem to go much more smoothly this time: while some still challenged their work, it was not halted and the new Persian king, Darius, was supportive. He even offered them financial help and threatened to punish anyone who disrupted what they were doing!

Clearly the words of Haggai and Zechariah were vital in stirring up faith and reminding the Jews of the task before them. They offered much more than a pep talk, though. What they said was particularly powerful because it was inspired by God. Hence, when the Jews acted on their prophecies, the miraculous happened and what had been impossible before now just came together. This reflects the importance of being open to God's words and guidance, for these transformational situations.

But how can we hear God without a Haggai or Zechariah to tell us what he is saying? The Holy Spirit that prompted their prophecies lives within all Christians, so God can speak to us too. Often this will not be in dramatic ways but through simple things, like thoughts that pop into our heads when we are praying, the counsel of wise friends that seems to ring true or Bible verses and Christian books that speak into our situations. Do we expect God to speak to us and are we listening when he does?

Consider using a notebook to jot down any thoughts that may be prompted by God. You can use this to direct your prayers and as a reminder to consider those thoughts further and test whether they really are of God.

CAROLINE FLETCHER

Saying thank you

Then the people of Israel – the priests, the Levites and the rest of the exiles – celebrated the dedication of the house of God with joy. (NIV)

Do you focus upon life's negatives or its positives? I must admit, I am more likely to focus on the former. If I had finished building the temple after decades of hard work and setbacks, I suspect I'd have been greatly relieved but would also have grumbled about how long it had taken and how difficult it had been. I might also have been frustrated that my temple wasn't as grand as the one it replaced, King Solomon's. He had been immensely wealthy, but those who returned from exile were not, so their temple was humbler. There was also much work still to be done: the city walls were in desperate need of repair. I'd have been tempted to rush into fixing those rather than stopping to take time to appreciate what had already been achieved.

However, the returnees did stop, gave thanks and celebrated this significant milestone. Indeed, they put real effort into marking this event – look at the numbers of animals they sacrificed. By marking the Passover, they not only took the time to celebrate the good things God had done for them recently, but also remembered the great things he had done in the past. The Passover festival commemorated their deliverance out of Egypt into the land God had promised them. In fact, Passover had even more significance for them now because God had restored them to that land once again, demonstrating that his promises are unbreakable.

Do we take time to thank God for the good things? It's easy not to amid life's busyness and problems. Yet showing our appreciation to God not only honours him but also builds up our faith. It reminds us of all he has done for us and helps us to trust him for the future. Do we need to thank God more?

'Every good and perfect gift is from above, coming down from the Father of the heavenly lights, who does not change like shifting shadows' (James 1:17). What good gifts can you thank God for?

CAROLINE FLETCHER

Don't forget love

This Ezra came up from Babylon. He was a teacher well versed in the Law of Moses, which the Lord, the God of Israel, had given. (NIV)

Today's reading is the first time we hear anything about Ezra. Despite only being mentioned in the later chapters of the book, he was clearly very important. Ezra was significant because he was a teacher of the law of Moses. Have a look at how many times his expertise in the law is mentioned in this chapter: it's a lot! His knowledge was clearly key to why he journeyed to Jerusalem to join the other Jews.

Ezra was concerned that although those who had returned before him had achieved a great deal in rebuilding the temple and re-establishing the sacrificial system, they had neglected other aspects of the law of Moses. This law includes the ten commandments that we are familiar with, but also scores of other regulations that you can read about in the first five books of our Old Testament. Ezra believed that attending the temple and offering sacrifices to God was not enough – people's behaviour had to change too.

And Ezra has a point, doesn't he? It's easy to fall into the trap of thinking that being a Christian is just about church attendance and failing to see the connection between our faith and how we treat others. While we as Christians no longer follow every regulation and ritual in the law of Moses, the New Testament teaches us that we fulfil its requirements by loving one another (Romans 13:8; Galatians 5:14). How well are we doing that?

Similarly, Jesus taught that we should love others as we love ourselves (Mark 12:31). Loving ourselves might seem self-centred, but if we treat ourselves badly, this often affects how we treat others. If, for instance, we push ourselves too hard, we tend to expect too much from others also. How well are you doing at loving yourself?

Is there anyone you struggle to love, whether yourself or someone else? Remember God is love, and we need his help to show compassion and care for those we find difficult, so ask the Lord to help.

CAROLINE FLETCHER

Putting God first

'We have been unfaithful to our God by marrying foreign women from the peoples around us.' (NIV)

Today's reading is an uncomfortable one. A significant number of those who returned from exile appear to have married local non-Jewish women. This disturbed Ezra because these women worshipped pagan fertility gods, and he believed they would influence their Jewish husbands to do likewise. As a result of his concerns, the Jewish leaders decided to tell these men to divorce their wives and expel them and their children from the community.

If we reflect upon the unique circumstances these Jews were in, we can better understand why they acted so harshly. The Jews who returned to Jerusalem were outnumbered by those around them who worshipped pagan gods. If their faith had become watered down through contact with these people, who would be left to proclaim the truth that there is only one true God? Everyone would be worshipping idols made of wood and stone and be following the immoral practices of these cults, such as religious prostitution and even child sacrifice.

It's important to look at the teaching of the Bible as a whole when deciding how to apply this passage today. In the New Testament, Paul tells Corinthian Christians that having an unbelieving partner is no reason for divorce (1 Corinthians 7:12–14). This suggests that what happened in Ezra's time was only necessary because of the particular situation the returnees faced and is not to be copied today. What is still relevant, however, is how seriously the returnees took their faith: they were not going to let anything get in the way of following God.

What hinders our commitment to God today: being distracted by money and possessions; worrying about what others think; time pressures; doubts and fears? Each of us faces different temptations, obstacles and distractions. The question is how serious we are about addressing those things.

Dear Lord, you know what prevents me from wholeheartedly following you. Help me to see what those things are and give me the strength and motivation I need to overcome them. Amen

CAROLINE FLETCHER

The parenthood of God

Hannah Fytche writes:

In the next two weeks, during which we will celebrate Father's Day, we will be spending time with biblical images and descriptions of God as our parent. Some of these images are gendered as either male or female; some are not, but rather elucidate a characteristic of who God is as our creator and the one who faithfully cares for us through every step of our lives. All of these images give us wonderful glimpses into the relationship with God that we are gifted through Jesus Christ: a relationship that gives us the identity of God's children, a relationship in which we are unconditionally loved and transformed by love.

My hope is that as you read each text, you will know God's unconditional love for you – you as you totally are – written deeply on your heart. Whatever your experience of parents, fathers or mothers – whether your own parents or someone else's, and whether good or damaging – I hope that you will encounter God afresh as the perfect parent.

God is the parent who loves you no matter what, risking all to draw you close. God is the parent who taught you to walk and who watches over your every footstep. God is the parent who brings out the best in who you are, calling you by name and calling you to new life, day by day.

So, then, let us begin with a prayer:

Creator God, you are the one who has formed me and made me your own – knitting me together in my mother's womb. You have called me by name: you know me intimately, as a parent knows the child they have brought up. As I dwell with descriptions of you as my parent, father or mother, may you draw me deeper into knowledge of your love for me. Amen

Carrying and sustaining

'Listen to me… you whom I have upheld since your birth, and have carried since you were born. Even to your old age and grey hairs I am he, I am he who will sustain you. I have made you and I will carry you; I will sustain you and I will rescue you.' (NIV)

I am writing these words in February 2021. At this point, the UK is in lockdown due to the Covid-19 pandemic. For eleven months I have been working at home and have endured emotional ups and downs of collective and personal grief, mixed with persevering hope for the pandemic's end.

Turning to write to you, then, I find myself confronted with these words from Isaiah in a powerful way. What incredible promises of faithfulness they are – particularly read in the context of a situation that has turned our world upside down.

We are those whom God has upheld since our birth. From the moment of our greatest vulnerability – the moment when we are born new to the world, crying with the shock of air in our lungs – God has carried us in safe hands. God has carried us through every vulnerability and change since then: through grief and recovery, trauma and new life, uncertainty and confidence, fear and joy. We're here, and God has been with us.

Even to our oldest age, God will sustain us. When our strength fails, God will sustain. When the earthly lives we've lived are behind us, God will sustain. We will see that he has never left us: safe hands have always been carrying us. God has been giving us breath, hope and assurance of love.

This I have known as everything has changed: that the parenthood of God is unchanging. God has faithfully carried me, protecting and providing for me with the love by which I was born. Throughout the pandemic, I have been given strength for today and hope for tomorrow.

Look back, if you can, over your experiences of recent years. How can you see God's faithfulness carrying you? What does this show you about the character of God's parenthood?

Sustaining and carrying God, thank you that your hands have encircled me since the day of my birth. May I trust that they encircle me still until the day of my death, ever leaning on the promises of your love. Amen

HANNAH FYTCHE

Teaching to walk

'It was I who taught Ephraim to walk, taking them by the arms; but they did not realise it was I who healed them... To them I was like one who lifts a little child to the cheek, and I bent down to feed them.' (NIV)

Do you remember learning to walk? I don't – unsurprisingly, as most babies learn to walk between six and 18 months, and adults can only recall memories from three to four years of age.

Despite being unable to remember learning to walk, many of us will have a picture in our minds of a parent, or someone like a parent, holding our tiny hands in theirs. We'll imagine them bearing our weight and holding us upright as we take our first wobbling steps. We'll notice how trusting this is, and how dependable those parent-figures in our life were to us when we were just learning to move for ourselves.

This is the metaphor that the prophet Hosea chooses to describe God. Writing in God's voice, Hosea portrays God as one who bears Ephraim's – God's people's – wobbling weight as they first learn to move on their own. God is like that dependable parent in whom the child trusts without realising it – and without being able to remember it when they are full grown. They cannot remember all those moments of being parented – the many mealtimes, the being lifted to their parent's cheek in affection and love, the first wobbly steps.

It is with lament that God is described as a parent here. God laments that their child has forgotten the thousand daily ways that they loved and nurtured them. This depiction of God's parenthood is part of the call to God's people to turn back to God, to imagine – even if they cannot remember – the ways that God has helped them to grow, causing them to trust him anew.

As we dwell with these images of God's parenthood, listen out for ways that they help you to see God's love by reminding you of the thousands of ways that God has helped you to grow.

Father God, you taught us to walk. You bore our weight as you showed us how to move on our own – how to live life in your way. Help us to remember and reimagine that image, that we may turn always back to you. Amen

HANNAH FYTCHE

Upholding with his hand

The Lord makes firm the steps of the one who delights in him; though he may stumble, he will not fall, for the Lord upholds him with his hand. (NIV)

We dwelt yesterday with the image of God as our parent teaching us to walk: our first wobbling steps were borne up by God. Today we read that it's not only those first steps, but every step since, that has been upheld by God.

This makes me think of my parents. In my 20s, I am independent. I live a couple of hours away from my family and I make my own decisions, yet my parents still uphold and support me. They are there on the other end of the phone. They share my joy and my sorrow. They have my back in difficult situations, reminding me of who I am and the values I hold – because they are my parents, and they know me and my story so well.

This is what God our parent does, too. God upholds our steps: as we move and grow, God is right there with us. God has our back: God knows our names and our stories, and God deeply affirms who we are in Christ. In this affirmation, God makes our footsteps firm. When we are reminded of who we are, we can keep living with confidence, integrity and authenticity whatever comes our way.

We all need this support at one time or another. We all need that encouragement from someone who knows us intimately. We know that this kind of person will tell us the truth, helping us to hold true to who we are and to grow in what we're good at. They will challenge and equip us to be our best selves, and they will be there for us in both our joy and our sorrow.

Whatever our relationships are like with our parents, we can all be held secure in the knowledge of God's parenthood. May this give you confidence for whatever you face today.

Write your name. As you look at your name, ask God to show you that he knows you by name. God is your parent, who taught you to walk and who has known you through every step. What affirmation does God speak over you?

HANNAH FYTCHE

Walking with

'When you pass through the waters, I will be with you; and when you pass through the rivers, they will not sweep over you. When you walk through the fire, you will not be burned; the flames will not set you ablaze.' (NIV)

Once a year I go to a beach with about 20 children and a group of other camp leaders. Part of our summer camp, this is always a glorious afternoon, digging the deepest holes, building the most intricate sandcastles and swimming out to sea.

One summer, I had the absolute joy of showing a seven-year-old the sea for the very first time. When they saw the sea, they were so amazed. They ran straight to the shore in their swim clothes – and sprung back, laughing, when the cold water touched their toes!

Once adjusted to the temperature, this child asked me to hold their hands as they went deeper and deeper. As waves came rolling in, I stood with my feet anchored in the sand and my hands holding this overjoyed child adrift. They kept their eyes on mine and could not stop giggling. Their eyes were so wide with wonder.

These verses from Isaiah remind me of this moment. Even though Isaiah's words are referring to dangerous situations from which God's people need rescuing, I can see in them resonances with my beach day. I, the responsible adult, was with the child as those waves rolled in, making it safe for them by holding them adrift. God our parent does the same with us as waves roll into our lives. Even in uncertain, new and uncontrollable circumstances, we can rely on God's hands to keep us adrift. We can keep our eyes fixed on God's – and we can even laugh at the joy of being safe with God, even while we're within the waves.

God, as our parent, is the one who ensures our safety – even in the waves and fire. Even when we're surrounded, God creates a spacious, safe place for us to be, to rest and to be held in his strong grip.

What is surrounding you? Where are the waves rolling in? Consider how God's hands are holding you even in their midst. Give thanks that he holds you, cares for you and makes you safe.

HANNAH FYTCHE

Watching over

He will not let your foot slip – he who watches over you will not slumber; indeed, he who watches over Israel will neither slumber nor sleep. The Lord watches over you – the Lord is your shade at your right hand; the sun will not harm you by day, nor the moon by night. (NIV)

Psalm 121 is one of my favourite psalms simply because, in the translation of the Bible I most often read, it contains the word 'slumber' twice. Isn't that glorious? God doesn't slumber; the Lord doesn't slumber.

Rather, God is awake through the watches of the night. Like a parent gazing over their sleeping child, God watches over each of us – watching us breathe as we sleep; watching worries and joys flicker under our dreaming eyelids; soothing us and making us safe when anxiety startles us awake.

God watches over us, and under his watchful gaze nothing is allowed to harm us. Not even the sun will harm us by day, not even the moon by night. Don't these words have a beautiful hint of a lullaby about them? You can imagine them being sung by a parent to a child as they sink into sleep and rest.

When I struggle to rest and sleep, these are some of the words I remember. They help me to imagine God as my parent, watching over me and keeping me safe while I get the rest that my mind and body needs. I can slumber because God doesn't. I can leave tasks undone at the end of the day because God's hands hold those unfinished tasks and God's eyes watch over me.

Even if harmful things do happen in my life, these words remind me that I can nevertheless rest in the midst of them. Even there, God watches over me. It's like God's watchful gaze stretches out a shelter around me, a resting-place where I know I am safe enough to relax and let my guard down before awakening to face the day, and whatever it holds, once more.

Thank you, God, that you watch over me. As I come to times of rest today, settle in me that deep sense of your presence and peace around me. May I lay down all that makes me anxious and be comforted by your love. Amen

HANNAH FYTCHE

Sheltering

Whoever dwells in the shelter of the Most High will rest in the shadow of the Almighty… He will cover you with his feathers, and under his wings you will find refuge; his faithfulness will be your shield and rampart. (NIV)

This is a psalm that I know deeply. It's the psalm I've prayed many times during Compline, night prayer – most memorably when I've been on retreat in a monastery in Assisi, Italy. Those of us on retreat gather in a dim but warm stone room and we pray these words at close of day.

To pray the psalm, we split into two groups and alternate saying each verse. We reflect to each other the amazing promises of God's protection and love, and they build up around us, layer upon layer of promises. My heart is settled into a place of refuge.

I imagine God's wings curving over me, bright feathers gathering me up into their protection and warmth. Inside those wings I find a spacious place where I can be honest with God; where I can breathe a little slower and let things go; where I can hear God's words of love and help sung over me. A space where I am loved without condition by the one who has made me and who knows me.

Praying these words with others helps me to see that I am not alone in this place of refuge – all of God's people are gathered under God's wings. All of his children are given this space of shelter from the bruises of busy, everyday life.

This is the kind of parent that God is: a parent who provides shelter for their children. We've seen that God our parent upholds us, even through fire and water, and watches over us through the night. Psalm 91 brings us another astonishing vision of what God is like: one who is strong and willing to protect those he has made, those who love God.

Which promise from this psalm do you shelter under today?

Lord, grow in me a childlike trust in the safety of your wings. Draw me to a place where I can be honest with you, knowing that as my parent you love me without condition. Your refuge will always be there for me. Amen

HANNAH FYTCHE

Longing to gather

'Jerusalem, Jerusalem, you who kill the prophets and stone those sent to you, how often I have longed to gather your children together, as a hen gathers her chicks under her wings, and you were not willing.' (NIV)

Jesus calls out these words as he sets his face towards Jerusalem and his journey to the cross. 'Children of Jerusalem,' he cries, 'God's created and loved people – you have turned away, and yet I long to gather you safe under my wings as a mother hen gathers her chicks.'

There are two movements in these words. First, there is the movement of God's people away from God; second, there is the movement of God, in the person of Jesus, towards God's people. The first movement is characterised by violent actions: killing, stoning and being resistant to God. The second movement is characterised by deep love – a mother's love – a love that unconditionally yearns for her children to be close to her.

Jesus' love is like this. It is unconditional: in love, Jesus, even seeing the violence of those he loves, longs to gather them close. He longs to shelter them under his wings and show them what it means to be loved again. He longs to heal them and to bring them back to life and goodness – to change their movement so that they are turning *towards* God once more.

It is for this love that Jesus sets his face towards Jerusalem. It is for this love that Jesus endures the cross. It is this love that brings him, and us, back to life.

It is by this love that we know we are forgiven. When I have needed forgiveness, for my own actions or for a situation I've been in, it is this love of Jesus that I encounter. When I pray for forgiveness, I find that I am met with a deep, reassuring sense of unconditional and transformative love. I am gathered to Jesus as a chick is gathered to a hen – his child, held safe, transformed.

Jesus, I confess to you the moments when I have moved away from you, in thoughts, actions and words. I ask that you gather me under your wings; I long to know your love. Amen

HANNAH FYTCHE

The Son revealing the Father (1)

The Word became flesh and made his dwelling among us. We have seen his glory, the glory of the one and only Son, who came from the Father, full of grace and truth… No one has ever seen God, but the one and only Son… has made him known. (NIV)

Over the past two days, we've dwelt with two images of God's sheltering, parenting wings over his children. One of these images referred to God as God was known in Old Testament times; the other was in the voice of Jesus, God-made-flesh dwelling among us.

In these verses from John, we read about how Jesus, God's Son, reveals the Father. The Son makes the character of the Father known – because the Son is the only one who has ever really seen the Father. By becoming God-with-us, Jesus is able to show us more and more what the parenthood of God is like – he is able to show us, for example, more of what it means for God to long to gather and shelter God's people under God's wings.

Jesus shows us that God is the kind of parent who will reach out to their children, running after them just to hold them close. God is the kind of parent who will travel the furthest distance to be near to his children and build a relationship with them – Jesus descends from heaven to walk the dusty earth with us, showing us in each step the love and glory of our Father from whom he came.

Draw near to Jesus, therefore. Through the person of Jesus, you'll get to know more and more of who the Father is, and what it means to be a child of God, given the right to become a child of the one who created all things, born of God.

Spend some time listening to Jesus' voice through the Bible and in prayer – for this reveals the voice of God the Father. Read stories from the gospels and imagine yourself into them. What does Jesus look and sound like? What is his character? What does this show you about the character of God, the Father, your parent?

Jesus, it is incredible that you reveal the Father to us. By becoming one of us, you bring heaven close – you bring the love of God our parent really close to me. Thank you. Amen

HANNAH FYTCHE

The Son revealing the Father (2)

The Son is the radiance of God's glory and the exact representation of his being, sustaining all things by his powerful word. After he had provided purification for sins, he sat down at the right hand of the Majesty in heaven.

'The radiance of God's glory': what an incredible description of Jesus. The word translated 'radiance' can also be translated 'brilliance' or 'effulgence' – all words which capture something of who Jesus is in relation to God. They show us that Jesus emanates the essence of God, the core of who God is.

Jesus reveals who God is, shining with the light of God's love and constant creativity. We saw this yesterday, imagining what Jesus reveals about the Father while he was on earth.

Today we see that Jesus, after the cross and resurrection, is at the right hand of God in heaven. From there he radiates God's glory and being, revealing who God is.

An example of how I've seen this is from a long summer vacation between university years. I'd been exhausted and had spent my summer sleeping. I was just starting to pray about and imagine the following months and years – praying about where God was calling me. I remember reading Luke 5:1–11, that familiar story of Jesus calling the disciples to become 'fishers of men'. As I reached that part – the pun in the tale – it was like I could hear Jesus laughing, catching my eye from the boat as I stood on the shore, wondering whether I should follow. In that laughter and catching of my eye, it was like Jesus was showing me that life with God is good because God delights.

I couldn't tell you whether that image of Jesus was my imagination or something more – a picture from God, leaping off scripture's pages to speak to me in that moment. But that image has stayed with me and given me courage to follow God as he has called me.

Jesus speaks to us still, revealing to us the Father's heart.

Jesus, thank you that you are alive! Thank you that you speak to us through scripture, prayer, listening and conversations. In so many ways you show us who God is and what God is like, giving us courage to follow. Amen

HANNAH FYTCHE

Made God's children

Because you are his sons, God sent the Spirit of his Son into our hearts, the Spirit who calls out, 'Abba, Father.' So you are no longer a slave, but God's child; and since you are his child, God has made you also an heir. (NIV)

By Jesus' death and resurrection we are redeemed into God's family. By the love of God, our creator and parent, Jesus died to bring us close – to gather us like a mother hen gathers her chicks. Now Jesus sits at God's right hand, reminding us that we are God's children.

This is what we've dwelt with over the past days. Today we see something new – the 'Spirit of the Son' whom God has sent into our hearts. This is the Holy Spirit. From our hearts she calls out an intimate name for God: 'Abba, Father'. We are caught up in the Spirit's cry – our hearts cry out too, like a child calling for their parent. Abba, Father.

We might not always be aware of this. Yet it is always happening, because God has made us his children. Even while we're asleep, the Spirit calls from our hearts, affirming us as God's children. Isn't this reassuring and beautiful?

Sometimes a harsh thought can creep in – that you're not praying or reading the Bible enough. Hear this: the Spirit is *always* calling out from within you. You don't have to do or pray 'enough', because God's Spirit is enlivening your heart to prayer even when you're not aware of it. In the same way that you don't stop being the child of your parents, you don't ever stop being a child of God.

This frees prayer to be a joyful joining in with the Spirit calling from within you. Listen for ways God is speaking from your heart – through your honest feelings; through words that bring you comfort and transformation. Pray by joining in with that cry of 'Abba, Father.'

As you say the words, dwell with the image of God as your Father. What does it mean? What challenge or encouragement comes with praying this prayer?

Abba, *Father.*

HANNAH FYTCHE

Living as God's child

Therefore, brothers and sisters, we have an obligation – but it is not to the flesh, to live according to it… For those who are led by the Spirit of God are the children of God… The Spirit himself testifies with our spirit that we are God's children. (NIV)

God makes us his children because of his unconditional love. This means that even while we were moving away from God – living lives that were destructive rather than creative, fearful rather than loving, sinful rather than free – God came in Jesus to make us God's children.

As God's children, we are given the Spirit within our hearts. This Spirit cries out in prayer, '*Abba*, Father.' This Spirit transforms us to live lives formed by God's love.

This is a wonderful thing. When we keep in step with the Spirit of God leading us, we will surely see new life spring up.

One year at summer camp, our Bible theme was 'fruits of the Spirit'. We focused on a fruit each day: love, joy, peace, patience, kindness, goodness, gentleness, faithfulness and self-control. We'd think about what each fruit could look like in our lives as we followed God, giving practical examples while making sure to communicate that the fruit grows because *God* makes it grow. It was amazing to see what the children already understood about each fruit, and the ways they spotted them growing in their own lives. It was also amazing to see in them the joy that God, not our own effort, makes the fruit grow.

It absolutely takes the pressure off of us when we remember that it's God's Spirit that causes these fruits to grow. We are freed to be God's children, delighting in him as we go and grow.

I wonder if there's a fruit that God is particularly growing in your life at the moment. You could consider what each fruit looks like in your life – and how God might be leading you in helping it to grow. Are there practical ways that you could join in with the Spirit's work?

Father, I am your child. Thank you that this means that your Spirit is at work within me as I follow you and get to know you. Show me how you are transforming me, bringing the fruits of the Spirit to life in my life. Amen

HANNAH FYTCHE

The Son praying to the Father

'Righteous Father, though the world does not know you, I know you, and they know that you have sent me. I have made you known to them, and will continue to make you known in order that the love you have for me may be in them and that I myself may be in them.' (NIV)

In John 17, just before his death on the cross, we read that Jesus prays to the Father – *and we get to read the content of his prayers*. We get to eavesdrop on the conversation between Jesus and God the Father, an intimate holy moment. Dwell with that: you get to eavesdrop on Jesus' prayers.

These are the words on God's heart, spoken from Son to Father. Jesus calls out: 'Father, may the love you have for me as your Son be written on to the hearts of all your children.' Jesus longs for this love to be written deep into our hearts, so that we may claim the identity we have been given as children of God.

When this love is written on to our hearts, we are affirmed and confirmed as the ones God has created and upheld, watched over and protected, known intimately, called and transformed to live in the best ways.

When this love is written on to our hearts, no other words hold any power over us. Lies can fall away: they don't need to stick to us or inform who we are. Others' opinions can be filtered through the love God has for us: we keep only what is true and let all else fall away.

When this love is written on to our hearts, we can be confident whatever comes our way. We are loved forever by God, who is our Father. No matter what we face, this love will last, and it will make us brave as we pursue what is good, even through times that are hard.

Hear this prayer prayed over you. Jesus has made the Father known and he continues to make the Father known. May the Father's love, which Jesus knows so well, be written on to your heart.

Father God, you love me. These are familiar words: let me hear them in a new way that allows me to claim my identity as your child afresh. May all else fall away as I hear you sing to my heart songs of your great love. Amen
HANNAH FYTCHE

Invited to pray to the Father

'This, then, is how you should pray: "Our Father in heaven, hallowed be your name, your kingdom come, your will be done, on earth as it is in heaven. Give us today our daily bread. And forgive us our debts, as we also have forgiven our debtors. And lead us not into temptation, but deliver us from the evil one."' (NIV)

Jesus teaches us how to pray. He gives us words for conversing with God our Father – the gift of language between parent and child. In these words there is a pattern for sharing what is on our hearts with God.

As a young child, I'd tell my parents the news of my day at bedtime. It would be little things, like pictures I'd drawn, and big things, like what I was worried about. My parents would listen, calming my worries and looking at my pictures.

As a teenager, I'd tell my parents about school, offloading everything – joys to griefs, with every drama too. My parents would listen and ask questions to help me see different perspectives and form how I would respond to things in the best ways. They'd tell me about their days, too. Now, I call my parents to tell them news – and I listen to their news, too. We talk about what's going on in our lives and share in each other's joys and sorrows.

At each of these times, I've had a language and pattern of talking with my parents. As I have grown up, I have grown in how I listen to and learn from them. Always, I have been thankful for their listening, wisdom and love. I wonder if we might experience the same with God our Father as we pray.

Sometimes we'll offload everything to God, asking for his help and wisdom. Sometimes we'll reflect more on other perspectives, and see that which we need to learn from and grow in. Sometimes we'll share and celebrate life with God and be thankful.

Jesus gives us a prayer which makes space for these things – for remembering God as our Father; for celebration; for asking for wisdom; for hearing God challenge our perspectives.

Pray the Lord's Prayer as Jesus has taught us. Imagine that you're talking with God as you'd talk with a parent or someone you trust and look up to. Does this change how you pray this prayer? How?

HANNAH FYTCHE

Dwelling with the Father

He said to me: 'It is done. I am the Alpha and the Omega, the Beginning and the End. To the thirsty I will give water without cost from the spring of the water of life. Those who are victorious will inherit all this, and I will be their God and they will be my children.' (NIV)

Reread today's passage – two or three times if you can. This is what is promised to us; this is the vision we have of the moment that God will gather, in love, all things into new life. Spend some time with the beauty of this vision.

God, seated on the throne, cries out with loud joy: 'Look! Look here, with your eyes wide open in wonder. I, God, dwell with my people. Every tear I will wipe away, for I am making everything new! Everything that was old or lost or broken or hurting, everything that was decaying or dying, everything that once was: I am now making it all new.'

Imagine that! A glorious new creation! This new creation includes water without limit for all who are thirsty, sustaining and refreshing all who drink it.

All who drink it: that is, those who inherit God's new creation, those who have been made his children. This is the vision we have of the moment when God will fully and finally gather up his children under his wings, holding them in the unconditional love of parent and creator.

As we finish our time dwelling on God's parenthood, take with you images of God's father- and motherhood – that encourage or challenge you to live in God's love and new life. If you need to, allow these images to heal damaging recollections of or relationships with parents you have known. Allow God the parent to breathe forgiveness and new life into them.

Above all, remember that you, created by God and adopted through Jesus into his family, are *loved and loved and loved and loved*. You are and ever will be a child of God, caught up into his new creation.

If you have paper and pen to hand, write or draw images for God's parenthood that have stuck with you across these two weeks. Pray: God, draw me close to you in the love you have for me as your creation and your child. Amen
HANNAH FYTCHE

Sisters united

Cham Kaur Mann writes:

If you were given the opportunity to meet someone in history, who would it be? A celebrity, a biblical character, a poet, an inventor or maybe a singer? Perhaps it would be a political figure, a mystic, a warrior or a sporting hero. What would you say to them and what would be your burning question? My mind would be filled with questions – 'Why did you…?', 'How did you…?', 'What if…?' I would follow all this with a request for any advice they'd be willing to offer. Now that I come to think about it, I have a huge gallery of people I'd like to meet, glean wisdom from and learn from.

Throughout this week, I plan to be totally self-indulgent! Yes, you heard correctly. I'm going to take a journey with a group of extraordinary women, sisters in fact, heroes of mine, and I'm inviting you to journey along with me. However, just to manage your expectations, they're not 'the usual suspects'. Neither are they celebrities, famous or, indeed, infamous! Yet in different seasons of my life, they have reappeared unexpectedly in conversations with friends, books I have read and through my personal reflections. Each time, they have left an indelible impression and inspired me to know them better and to be better myself.

The group of women I'm referring to are none other than Zelophehad's daughters. Numbers 27 informs us that their father had died without male heirs to inherit the apportioned plot of family land. In ancient Near Eastern culture, women were considered subordinate to men and typically treated as property, without rights to land ownership. As orphans without an inheritance, they would probably be left poor, destitute, homeless and without dowries. In addition, without male support they would be destined to lives of hardship and likely exploitation. Yet these desperate circumstances and the course of history were transformed by their bold and courageous act of speaking out on the matter.

I'm sure many of us find it much easier to advocate on behalf of others than for ourselves, and yet sometimes this is the only right and viable course of action. As we study this story in detail, perhaps you could be thinking about what you do when faced with unjust traditions, structures or systems.

Hidden *not* hidden

The daughters of Zelophehad son of Hepher, the son of Gilead, the son of Makir, the son of Manasseh, belonged to the clans of Manasseh son of Joseph. (NIV)

A few years ago, I watched the film *Hidden Figures* (if you haven't already done so, do watch it with friends or family). It tells the real-life story of African-American women mathematicians who play a vital role in the NASA space programme of the 1960s. The film focuses on how they made significant contributions while simultaneously overcoming barriers of race and gender. It's both an amazing and inspiring watch.

The term 'hidden figures' resonates with the story of the daughters of Zelophehad, who, up until Numbers 27, were hidden, unknown and never mentioned, even in relation to some other biblical figure. In one sense this is hardly surprising, as women in Old Testament cultures were seldom promoted and generally 'sentenced' to invisibility and life in the shadows.

There are many cultures and subcultures on our own doorsteps that still hold the belief that women and girls are best kept hidden. During the Covid lockdown, this was compounded for many women who faced multiple attempts at censure through abuse. However, perhaps somewhat ironically, we also witnessed a new degree of visibility, as female leaders on every continent gained recognition for bold, courageous and exemplary leadership in the face of the crisis. I have been greatly encouraged to stretch further in my own leadership as a result.

I believe we need to see and hear more women change-makers in our structures and systems, because ultimately everyone benefits from our diverse voices, wisdom, gifts and unique contributions.

Does the term 'hidden figure' apply to you in this season of life?

Lord God, thank you that you know us better than we know ourselves. Help us to identify barriers, internal and external, that confine us to places of hiddenness. Embolden us to fully embrace the work you have assigned to us. Amen
CHAM KAUR MANN

What is your name?

The names of the daughters were Mahlah, Noah, Hoglah, Milkah and Tirzah. (NIV)

I recall the agony of the first day of each school year. I used to dread the moment when the teacher called out the class register. The teacher would hesitate, look up and call out a strange version of my name. What made matters worse was the teasing and laughter that followed from the rest of the class. Embarrassed as I am to admit it, I remember telling someone at junior school that my name was Manjit (a very popular Sikh name at the time) because it was easier to pronounce. How terrible is that? The very name my father had thoughtfully given to me is actually a place of great historical significance for Sikhs – Chamkaur. Yet I found myself replacing it with a name that wasn't even my own, to avoid ridicule!

Names are interesting, aren't they? They can say so little about us and they can say so much. Some people and cultures choose names in honour of celebrities and personalities or because they simply like the sound of them. Others choose or create names in defiance of what oppressors have imposed upon them.

In my parents' culture, names reflect heritage, parental aspirations and the hope that children will somehow embody the traits and behaviours of the given name. Biblical name-giving follows similar principles. For example, Zelophehad's daughters' names may have conveyed the mood of their parents – or indeed the circumstances they faced: Mahlah means sickness or infirmity; Noah, timid or shaky; Hoglah, dancing or partridge; Milkah, queen and ruler; and Tirzah, beloved or favoured/pleasing one. As you will no doubt have noticed, the names became more hope-filled around the births of Milkah and Tirzah!

Names tell us something important about ourselves; they also tell us something about how we experience God. What names of God are particularly important to you right now?

Loving God, help us to see more of you as Abba (father), Jehovah-Jireh (the Lord our provider) and Jehovah-Shalom (the Lord is peace). Help us to reach out and call on your name. Amen

CHAM KAUR MANN

Location, location, location

The daughters of Zelophehad son of Hepher, the son of Gilead, the son of Makir, the son of Manasseh, belonged to the clans of Manasseh son of Joseph. (NIV)

Picture the scene: 'So, where are you from?' 'Birmingham,' I reply. 'No… where are you *really* from?' To which I then reply: 'Well, how far back to you really want me to go and, by the way, where are *you* really from?' This is fairly typical of many conversations I have had when some people meet me for the first time. No doubt the colour of my skin has something to do with it.

Our locations and our contexts matter. They matter because they shape us; they leave an indelible impression on us and a memory that continues to influence our ability to make sound choices and helpful decisions.

As a British South Asian Punjabi woman, I can appreciate many aspects of life from the perspective of our five sisters and something of their cultural context. I can imagine the influences, expectations and narratives they might have imbibed from birth, and I can almost hear the scripts they would have rehearsed. For these women, their roles would have been defined, assigned and prescribed. They would have been familiar with the pressure to conform and comply. They probably would have regularly heard references to family honour, dishonour and shame.

Cultural location is a particular defining factor, but their story comes to us from another kind of location, the borders of the so-called land of promise, which in that moment looked far from promising for them.

Yet it is precisely between the old thing and the new place, through the cultural and geographical locations, that God's 'new thing' emerges. Our five sisters become more than their background and history expects of them, and they enter a whole new location of possibilities.

How have your cultural and geographical location(s) helped your journey of personal growth?

Lord God, thank you for your desire to bring us into new places, even if our personal contexts have been challenging and limiting. Between our old thing and our new place, allow your new thing to emerge. Amen

CHAM KAUR MANN

Common concern

'Why should our father's name disappear from his clan because he had no son? Give us property among our father's relatives.' (NIV)

I recently filled out a census form for my household. Initially, I approached it with the attitude of 'What, again?' – until I realised that the last census had been taken ten years ago. I quickly appreciated its significance and that therefore I needed to take it seriously – not to mention the warning – or should I say 'incentive' – that failure to fill out the form could result in a £1,000 fine!

I realise that the census is important for all of us who live in the UK, as it helps to ensure that our communities get the services we need for the next ten years and beyond. It also helps to build a picture for local authorities and charities of where education, healthcare and transport funding needs to be allocated.

Similarly, Moses asked for a census to be carried out of each household to ensure the proper allocation of land to the people of Israel as they entered the promised land. This all made perfect sense, as he was keen to meet the needs of the community by distributing the land resources fairly. However, the information required for the census revealed a bias that disadvantaged our five sisters and women like them in their households.

Land and resource allocation was dependent upon having male heirs within the household. As we've already learned, the sisters' father had died, and they did not have a brother who could inherit the portion of land and therefore ensure security for them. They were caught between a rock and a hard place, so they approached Moses together, with their common concern, and made an appeal to him which raised questions about the fairness of this law!

As you ponder this story, think about the gaps which might disadvantage groups and communities in your area.

God of justice and mercy, we know that your heart and concern is always towards the vulnerable, such as widows, orphans, immigrants and the poor among us. Help us to share your concern for others. Amen

CHAM KAUR MANN

Cooperating together

They came forward and stood before Moses, Eleazar the priest, the leaders and the whole assembly at the entrance to the tent of meeting. (NIV)

The phrase 'teamwork makes the dream work' is a bit of a cliché, but I have worked in a few teams myself, so I know the gift of a 'dream team', as well as the challenges brought about by a dysfunctional team.

I appreciate being part of a group committed to working together in a spirit of cooperation, where each member wants the best outcome for all and people move in the power of 'we' and 'us', not in the gear of 'I, me, my'. I have been on the receiving end of the kind of blessing that Psalm 133 speaks about, which emerges when diverse voices, perspectives, skills and talents come together to solve problems.

I try to imagine the sisters' strategy when faced with the census news – the future looked bleak, there was little hope on the horizon, and yet… You've heard the phrase 'two heads are better than one' – imagine five heads, five amazing women on your team, bringing together their different skills, knowledge and wisdom. Imagine them refining their case, ensuring that their words would be clear, leaving no room for misinterpretation.

The fact that they were able to challenge as they did suggests they'd done their homework and gathered the appropriate evidence to bolster their case. At some level, they complemented each other's strengths – perhaps the creative thinker stood alongside the strategist and the operations lead alongside the spokesperson. They would undoubtedly be aware of the high stakes involved in stepping out, speaking up and taking such radical action. For example, they could have been interpreted as disrespecting the leadership, or even as troublemakers bringing dishonour to their father's name. If nothing else, they risked being ostracised from the community and eternally labelled (and not in a good way!).

What unique gifts do you carry and how do they need to be amplified?

Lord God, guide us and lead us as we work with others. Help us to remember that we each have unique gifts to contribute to the whole. Amen

CHAM KAUR MANN

Making the ask

They came forward and stood before Moses, Eleazar the priest, the leaders and the whole assembly at the entrance to the tent of meeting.

I love watching football – just ask my housemate! She swiftly exits the room whenever a match is on, as I all too frequently volunteer an uninvited running commentary on the team's performance. It usually goes along the lines of: 'Pass the ball! Get a move on! Now, if I were on the pitch, I could kick the ball with my eyes closed!' The truth is, of course, I couldn't. My housemate will also readily testify that I have a poor relationship with coordination.

By deciding to leave their tent, our sisters were effectively stepping away from the security of their comfort zone. It was all well and good debating, discussing and complaining within the confines of their home, but taking action would mean that they risked everything. In taking their next steps, they allowed God to create opportunities that otherwise wouldn't have existed. They were about to present a landmark proposal that could go either way, and they needed the influencers and gatekeepers to rally to their cause. They needed allies – people who would listen, take them seriously and be prepared to use their privilege and influence on behalf of the disenfranchised and marginalised sisters.

In this scenario, Moses' response would be critical to their future. Notably, instead of being dismissive, getting defensive, retreating into tradition (i.e. 'We've always done it this way'), publicly shaming them or claiming to be the fount of *all* knowledge, Moses does the unexpected: he takes the matter seriously and seeks God's wisdom on their behalf. Such a question had simply never been raised before in relation to the law and custom.

When we assume that the way things are is the way God wants them to be, these sisters (and Moses) reveal the wisdom of simply making the ask. Is there an 'ask' you need to make of God or someone else in your life today?

CHAM KAUR MANN

Change-makers

So Moses brought their case before the Lord, and the Lord said to him, 'What Zelophehad's daughters are saying is right. You must certainly give them property as an inheritance among their father's relatives and give their father's inheritance to them. Say to the Israelites, "If a man dies and leaves no son, give his inheritance to his daughter."' (NIV)

I recall a number of situations where I've either had to stand alone in defence of what felt was right or been among the few speaking out against injustice in particular circles. I have to admit, in my earlier years this was an incredibly scary experience, as I was often in a place of disadvantage, like the proverbial underdog.

It *always* takes tremendous courage to stand up to people who appear to idolise tradition and are resistant to new perspectives and ways of doing things. The decision to speak out in such circumstances can feel overwhelming and intimidating. Such feelings are often compounded by a lack of resources and power, making it even harder to progress the cause.

Yet throughout both biblical and world history, situations constantly emerge which demand that someone, somewhere, be prepared to stand up, speak out and do whatever it takes to make a difference. Individuals have been prepared to boycott, stay seated on a bus, go to prison or even die for a cause so that justice can be upheld.

Together, these sisters made a difference that impacted on women's inheritance rights. Although they secured women's inheritance rights, it's likely that pervasive marital customs within the patriarchal system would have overruled these fairly quickly. One step forward, two steps back. Yet, our five sisters remind us of what should be done and could be done simply because it's the right thing to do. Their actions have been recorded in the Bible and are therefore available to inspire many of us to take action against all odds. Quite simply, they invite us to become the change-makers of today.

Lord God, we thank you for change-makers in scripture. We thank Jesus, the ultimate change-maker. Help us to make a difference in the lives of those around us and those we will never meet. In Jesus' name. Amen

CHAM KAUR MANN

Naomi: a story of hope

Jackie Harris writes:

The book of Ruth must be among the most read and well-loved parts of the Bible. While on the surface it is a simple narrative, short and easy to read, there is treasure upon treasure to be found when we explore some of the many themes woven through this story of two women who find themselves in a desperate situation.

The book takes its name from Ruth, but it is very much Naomi's story, and it seems to me that she is one of the unsung heroes of the Bible. While everyone extols the virtues of Ruth, Naomi gets a mixed response. Some have described her as an embittered old woman who lost her faith and manipulated her daughter-in-law in order to secure her own future; but others see in Naomi a profound figure of faith and a caring and gracious mother-in-law. I am firmly in the latter category and believe there is much we can learn from both her character and her story.

I suggest reading the whole book before we begin. It's such an accessible story and having an overview will be helpful as we focus on Naomi and how she responds to the changes and challenges she faces.

At first glance, it may seem that God is not particularly involved in the story. There are only two occasions when God is described as directly intervening in events: first, when he comes to the aid of his people by providing food for them (Ruth 1:6) and, second, when he enables Ruth to have a son (Ruth 4:13). But as we look more closely, we can see God's loving kindness to Naomi and how he is at work, often in ordinary circumstances and through ordinary people.

This is what encouraged me when I happened to be reading the book of Ruth during a period of loss. My circumstances were different, but, like Naomi's, my future suddenly looked uncertain, and I felt very vulnerable. As I followed her narrative, I found fresh hope and courage as I saw how God worked in her life and blessed her in unexpected ways.

I hope that as we study her story in depth, we will be encouraged to be more alert to how God is working in our lives day by day.

Far from home

There was a famine in the land. So a man from Bethlehem in Judah, together with his wife and two sons, went to live for a while in the country of Moab. (NIV)

Naomi's story begins with a family upheaval. There is famine in the land and so they leave their home in Bethlehem and move to Moab. On first reading, it sounds reasonable, and I must admit I assumed that Elimelek was simply looking out for his family at a difficult time. But as I dug a little deeper, a different picture emerged.

This family lived in Bethlehem, in the land promised to God's people, but they chose to go to Moab, a place where God was not honoured and where it would be difficult to remain faithful to him and obey his laws. Moreover, Jewish tradition suggests that Elimelek was a leader with responsibilities in the community. Famine in the land was usually seen as a sign of God's punishment (Leviticus 26:14–16), so the right course of action would have been to stay and to encourage the people to turn back to God.

Commentators suggest that in taking the initiative to go to Moab, Naomi's husband stepped out of the will of God. Certainly in marrying Moabite women her sons disobeyed the law, which forbade marriage outside the Jewish nation.

Suddenly these opening verses begin to sound challenging. How do we respond to difficulties or setbacks? Might we be guilty of moving out of the will of God because it's become more taxing or inconvenient?

Naomi, of course, may not have had any say in the decision to leave Bethlehem or in her sons' choice of brides, but now, with her life turned upside down, she has to make a choice about what to do next. She hears that food is once again plentiful in Israel, that God is blessing his people, and she decides to retrace her steps and return home. It proves to be a wise decision.

Being where God wants us is not always comfortable, but it is always the safest place to be. Is there a decision you need to make today?

JACKIE HARRIS

Beloved mother-in-law

'Where you go I will go, and where you stay I will stay. Your people will be my people and your God my God.' (NIV)

I have known quite a few women who had difficult relationships with their mothers-in-law, but this doesn't seem to have been a problem for Ruth and Orpah. This famous passage and the conversation between Naomi and her daughters-in-law reveals a genuine bond of love between these women who, having grieved together, now seek to build a new life in the land of Judah. But then Naomi has second thoughts and urges Ruth and Orpah to return to their families, believing this to be their best option.

I am struck by Naomi's generosity of spirit here. These two young women must have been a comfort to her, but she is willing to put their needs first and seek what she believes to be best for them. Despite her grief and the gravity of her own situation, she blesses them, prays for them and tries to make them see that they have more chance of a future without her. It can't have been an easy decision. What a lovely woman!

Both Ruth and Orpah protest. Both are willing to leave behind everything and everyone they know to accompany Naomi to an unknown future in a foreign nation. What was it about Naomi that inspired such loyalty? Her name means 'pleasant' or 'charming', and perhaps it was a name that suited her character.

However, I think Ruth's insistence tells us more. She wants to make her home among Naomi's people and to know Naomi's God. Something about the way Naomi lived her life must have made an impression on these two young women.

In the end, Orpah reluctantly returned to Moab, but Ruth continues on the road to Bethlehem and a new life. What she has learnt about and from Naomi beckons her on.

Father, help me to see beyond my needs to the needs of others and to live in a way that will draw others to you. Amen

JACKIE HARRIS

Blinded by grief

'Don't call me Naomi,' she told them. 'Call me Mara, because the Almighty has made my life very bitter.' (NIV)

The arrival of Naomi and Ruth causes quite a stir in Bethlehem, and the women who knew her barely recognise her. I wonder if this is not so much her physical appearance, but her demeanour, for Naomi gives herself a new identity – Mara, meaning bitter. The contrast between the meaning of her name – pleasant – and the person she has become – disappointed, empty and seemingly abandoned by God – is unbearable for her. At this point in the story, Naomi cannot see beyond her loss and grief. The spark of hope that led her back to Bethlehem appears to have disappeared. Perhaps being back in her hometown is too painful a reminder of all that she has lost.

What Naomi doesn't yet realise is that God is at work. Ruth and Naomi have returned 'as the barley harvest was beginning' (1:22) and Ruth is able to take advantage of the Jewish tradition of gleaning, which allowed the poor to gather the leftover grain in the fields. More than that, it just so happens that the field where she is working belongs to Boaz, a distant relative of Naomi's husband. Quietly, and for the moment unrecognised, God is working his purposes out.

It's hard to look beyond our circumstances sometimes, isn't it? Often it is only as we look back that we can see how God made a way for us: bringing the right people into our lives, providing unexpected resources or encouragements, guiding us to the right place at the right time, enabling us to develop skills, etc.

Naomi's story encourages us to trust that God is at work in our lives too. He can change any situation. Hold on to that thought today.

Think back over difficult periods in your life. Can you see where God made a way for you and turned things around? Pray with David: 'I am trusting you, O Lord… My future is in your hands' (Psalm 31:14–15, NLT).

JACKIE HARRIS

Full of thanksgiving

'Where did you glean today? Where did you work? Blessed be the man who took notice of you!' (NIV)

I wonder how Naomi spent the day while Ruth was working in the fields. She had agreed to let her go, but perhaps not without some misgivings. Verse 22 suggests that gleaning could be a dangerous occupation for a woman alone. She must have worried about her, but Ruth's return dispels her fears.

Naomi is amazed at the amount of grain Ruth brings home and overjoyed to hear about her experiences. She immediately recognises Boaz as a relative and expresses her gratitude with words of blessing. In fact, Boaz was not only a relative, but also one of their guardian-redeemers. The Hebrew word for this is a legal term for one who has the obligation to redeem a relative in serious difficulty (Leviticus 25:25–55).

This is another example of God's provision through laws he established long ago, and it is a turning point for Naomi. With food to eat, a safe place for Ruth to work and a kind relative nearby, her bitterness is subdued, and fear gives way to thankfulness.

We hear a lot now about the importance of gratitude and being thankful. Indeed, they are recognised as key factors for both our mental and physical health. This is because when we practise gratitude, we increase the amount of dopamine in the brain, which is the thing that makes us feel good. But it is not limited to just good times. Gratitude is defined as the quality of being thankful and the readiness to show appreciation and to return kindness. This is the quality we see in Naomi, and it opens the way for change not only in her life, but also in the lives of those around her.

'It is only in this expressing of gratitude for the life we already have that we discover the life we've always wanted' (Ann Voskamp, author of One Thousand Gifts*). What might you give thanks for today?*

JACKIE HARRIS

Agent of change

'My daughter, I must find a home for you, where you will be well provided for.' (NIV)

While Boaz has been generous and gone the extra mile to ensure the women have enough to eat, the long-term future for Naomi and Ruth remains uncertain. With few options open to them, Naomi sets out an audacious plan. Up to now, she has been the receiver; it has been Ruth who has taken the initiative and gone out to work. But now we see Naomi the giver, using her knowledge of her culture and what she has learned of Boaz to give back and to secure a future for Ruth.

In effect Naomi is seeking to answer her own prayer in chapter 1, when she prayed that Ruth would find a 'home'. The word used there means rest or contentment – through a husband (1:9). Here (in verse 1), she uses the same word for home. Back in chapter 1, she could see no way of answering her prayer for Ruth, and their situation seemed hopeless; but now she sees things differently, and she is going to do all she can to help.

I have heard more than one preacher suggest that when we don't know what to do, we should try to discern what God is doing and join in. I hope I am not stretching things too far in suggesting that this is exactly what we see Naomi doing here. Sensing God at work through Boaz, she determines to play her part. Clearly an organiser, she assesses the situation, sees an opportunity and presents a clear plan of action to Ruth.

This story is a wonderful account of how God works through faithful people to fulfil his purposes for them. How does God want to work through you today? What do you sense God doing in your life or the lives of those around you, and how might you join in?

Father, I want to be among your faithful people. Help me to discern what you want to do in my life and in the lives of those I love, and to work with you to fulfil your purposes. Amen

JACKIE HARRIS

Trusting in God's provision

Then Naomi said, 'Wait, my daughter, until you find out what happens. For the man will not rest until the matter is settled today.' (NIV)

Waiting – so much of life seems to involve waiting. Sometimes it is a happy expectation: the child waiting for Christmas or a birthday, the penfriend waiting for a letter, the couple waiting for the birth of a child. Sometimes the waiting is more anxious: waiting for the results of an exam, hospital tests or an interview. More often, waiting is simply a chore: waiting in a queue, for a delivery or for a reply to a query.

At this point in the story, Naomi is waiting to see what will happen, and her words to Ruth suggest a calm confidence. Naomi understands God's laws about land ownership and the responsibilities of the kinsman-redeemer, and she sees God's provision in Boaz. She also knows that she can trust Boaz to do the right thing and that he will act quickly. Commentators suggest that the gift of grain Boaz gave Ruth to take back to Naomi (3:17) would be understood as not simply a gift of food, but also as a symbol of his promise to meet her other need, for a child through Ruth to continue the family line.

So Naomi and Ruth must wait, but they can wait with hope because their kinsman-redeemer is working for them.

In our own times of waiting – whether anxious, expectant or simply frustrating – let's learn from Naomi. What can we see of God's goodness in the people around us, in the society in which we live and the place we find ourselves? We, of course, have a supreme redeemer in Jesus. We have his promise that he will never leave us (Matthew 28:20), and scripture tells us that he intercedes for us (Romans 8:34). Can we wait with a quiet confidence, knowing we can trust him to act for us?

Lord, it is so hard sometimes not to worry about how things will turn out or not to try to rush things. Please help me to trust you in the waiting. Amen
JACKIE HARRIS

Unexpected blessings

The women said to Naomi: 'Praise be to the Lord, who this day has not left you without a guardian-redeemer… He will renew your life and sustain you in your old age.' (NIV)

And so Naomi steps into a new future, with a new family and a rich life to look forward to. God has given her more than she could have expected and in unexpected ways.

The women who gather around Naomi rejoice with her and list the blessings they see in her life. She has a family who will care for her in her old age, a loving daughter-in-law and now a child who, according to Israelite law, would be counted as a descendant of Naomi, so the family line is saved from extinction. What a transformation they have witnessed! Naomi has moved from emptiness to fullness, and from poverty and sorrow to security and joy.

Looking back on Naomi's story, we can see how the choices she made – to return to Bethlehem, to let Ruth accompany her, to be thankful and to provide a secure future for Ruth – enabled her to experience more and more of God's goodness and care.

Perhaps we are longing to see a transformation in our life or in the lives of people we care for. Can we take courage from Naomi's experience? How might God want to work through us to answer those prayers?

But the story doesn't end here. The short genealogy which ends the book of Ruth explains how Naomi's grandson became grandfather to King David, Israel's shepherd king, and an ancestor of Jesus. So Naomi's story is part of a much bigger story. This is so encouraging. It's one of many examples in the Bible of how God works through ordinary people, even those who appear hopeless, to bring about his purposes.

God wants to work through our lives too, however unpromising they might appear. Remember Naomi: her story is a beautiful example of how God can turn a hopeless situation into something glorious.

Heavenly Father, we are filled with wonder as we see your graciousness in the life of Naomi. Help us to discern your goodness in our lives and to trust in your redeeming power. Amen

JACKIE HARRIS

Letters to the seven churches

Michele D. Morrison writes:

At the end of John's gospel, he records an exchange between Jesus and Peter, as Jesus restores the disciple who had let him down spectacularly during his trial. Having confessed his love for Jesus, Peter is then confronted with the stark image of his own future martyrdom. He notices John and asks about his future prospects. Jesus replies curtly, 'If I want him to remain alive until I return, what is that to you?' (John 21:22, NIV). A rumour spreads that John won't die, a rumour John doesn't believe.

I wonder if, years later, John thought about that rumour when he was banished to the island of Patmos and drawn into the visions described in the book of Revelation. The visions are so vivid he must have felt he had stepped into another realm of reality. They are visions which he, the beloved disciple with a gift for writing, was entrusted to impart to Jesus' followers.

'On the Lord's Day I was in the Spirit,' John writes (Revelation 1:10). In the solitude and silence of banishment, John lives close to God. He describes the awesome appearance of Jesus and records his words to him: 'Write, therefore, what you have seen, what is now and what will take place later… The seven lampstands are the seven churches' (Revelation 1:19–20).

The dramatic visions of Revelation begin with letters to seven churches in Asia Minor, modern-day Turkey. In a style reminiscent of the way Jesus rooted his parables in circumstances familiar to his audience, each letter is tailored to the locations and circumstances of the recipients.

The letters, dictated by Jesus, are actually addressed to the angel of each church. Jesus expects his serving angels to pass on the messages. Does he suspect his churches might not be listening, though? Belt and braces, he instructs John to write the messages down.

What about us, today? Is your church sensitive to the voice of Jesus? Would you recognise if Jesus had moved on?

The first notes I wrote ten years ago for *Day by Day with God* were about sharing our faith, and looked at the way the first church shared their faith as recorded in Acts. Over this next week, we'll look at the report cards of seven of these first churches, as given by Jesus himself, and challenge ourselves to consider what he might write to us, today.

'Recalculating...'

'I know your deeds, your hard work and your perseverance… Yet I hold this against you: you have forsaken the love you had at first.' (NIV)

The navigator of a ship must be meticulous, constantly checking the ship's position against the stars. If she is slightly out in her calculations, the ship will not reach its destination.

The church in Ephesus had lost sight of the Lighthouse. The beam of love for Jesus had died, and they were navigating blind. How could they recover the divine perspective, calibrated to align with Jesus? 'Repent and do the things you did at first,' Jesus exhorts (v. 5).

What does first love do? It sings the praises of the beloved. It is focused, struggling to think of anything else but the beloved. A church in love with Jesus is a worshipping church. Worship lifts believers into the presence of Jesus, where vision and understanding can be recalibrated, where minds and spirits are transformed and renewed. 'Consider how far you have fallen!' (v. 5).

What I missed most during the Covid-19 lockdowns was corporate worship. Zoom services provided a good platform for teaching, preaching, conveying news and even enabling personal contact through 'break-out rooms'. But I found it difficult to connect with my church family in spiritually alive worship. As I write, I am eagerly anticipating the day when, as gathered church, we can lose ourselves in adoration, praise and love of our Saviour.

The church at Ephesus is commended for testing those who claim to be apostles, identifying the real ones and weeding out the fakes. Worship clarifies our vision as the Spirit enables our understanding. Our cultural atmosphere in the 21st century is fogged with claims that there are 'many truths'. As Jesus-followers, we are called to be meticulous in calibrating our understanding of the truth by the words and actions of Jesus.

The love of Jesus is the lodestar that will guide us all home.

Lord Jesus, set our hearts on fire for you. Show us how to worship as church, so that we are sure and accurate in identifying truth. Amen

MICHELE D. MORRISON

Hold on!

'I know your afflictions and your poverty – yet you are rich! I know about the slander of those who say they are Jews and are not, but are a synagogue of Satan.' (NIV)

By the world's standards, the church in Smyrna is poor. Already enduring persecution, Jesus warns them of a tsunami of further trouble to come. Stay faithful, he says. The end is in sight.

It seems there was a cohort of Jews who were putting out lies about the church. It's hard not to retaliate when slandered, especially if the name of Jesus is brought into disrepute. Placards proclaiming 'Jesus is my Saviour' in the hands of violent rioters storming the US Capitol building in 2021 blasphemed the name of Jesus. Followers of the Prince of Peace do not wield nooses and machine guns. How should true believers react? 'Remain faithful,' Jesus says. By living out lives of mercy and sacrificial love, a watching world will see Jesus, not a caricature of him.

To identify as Christian today can lead to assumptions that one is affiliated with a certain political agenda. I have sympathy for those identifying as Red-Letter Christians, who stand by the words of Jesus as recorded in scripture and preach humility, mercy and justice.

To understand truth, as we saw yesterday, we need to stay close to him who is truth. Perhaps the Jews of Smyrna thought they were telling the truth. Saul, before his dramatic conversion, thought he was upholding the truth. Those who stormed the Capitol, those who adhere to conspiracy theories today, believe they have the truth.

The unbelieving world sees a church divided perhaps as never before. Real Jesus followers are on their knees crying out to God to reveal himself through the church's loving actions as well as its words. What does Jesus say? Be faithful. Stand firm.

Jesus warned, 'Watch out that no one deceives you. For many will come in my name' (Matthew 24:4–5).

Sit with these thoughts for some time. Ask God to show you anything you are believing which does not accord with the truth. Act on that.

MICHELE D. MORRISON

Where do you spend your time?

'I know where you live – where Satan has his throne. Yet you remain
true to my name. You did not renounce your faith in me, not even in
the days of Antipas, my faithful witness, who was put to death in your
city – where Satan lives.' (NIV)

There is something profoundly personal in someone knowing where you
live. Twice in this letter, God confirms that he knows not just the address,
but also the nature of the Pergamum postcode.

The believers in Pergamum lived in an empire which demanded
emperor worship and encouraged and enabled immoral expressions of
veneration of idols. Some believers remained faithful to Jesus, even in
the face of death. But others compromised God's truth, ensnared by the
culture in which they lived: a culture where Satan had his throne. 'Repent,'
Jesus says.

Jesus invites us to live in his neighbourhood, to sit down at his right
hand. This starts as an act of the will and ends as a desire of the heart.
Without God, we can do nothing. Without his Spirit, we cannot even distin-
guish good from evil. We see in shades of grey. We need Jesus every hour
to help us live in the world but not become of the world.

The double-edged sword in the mouth of Jesus separates black from
white, good from evil. Relying on Jesus can keep us from settling down
in the bad neighbourhoods. The love of Jesus can enable the church uni-
versal to present a united and consistent theology to a watching world –
where Satan has his throne.

What's the atmosphere of your neighbourhood – not necessarily your
address, but the place you spend most of your time? In the digital life of the
21st century, do you hang out in virtual neighbourhoods where Satan has
his throne? Do you get trapped in the vicious one-upmanship cul-de-sac of
Facebook? Do you join in the sharp cliffhanger tweets on Twitter? Are you
lost in the dark tunnels of porn? God knows where we hang out. He can
send the removal van, if we ask him.

---

*Next time you're queuing for coffee or groceries, don't pull out your phone.
Engage with the person behind you. Let her glimpse God's neighbourhood
of kindness and love.*

MICHELE D. MORRISON

Turning a blind eye

'I have this against you: you tolerate that woman Jezebel, who calls herself a prophet. By her teaching she misleads my servants into sexual immorality and the eating of food sacrificed to idols.' (NIV)

Thyatira was a commercial centre where trade guilds held a lot of power. The guilds hosted frequent feasts, perhaps monthly, and these celebrations included emperor worship and sexual immorality. One's livelihood could depend on one's participation in the guild associated with one's trade, so Christians had stark choices to make which impacted on their economic success.

It appears that in the midst of this active church, commended for its love, faith, service and perseverance, there is a temptation to compromise with the guilds' activities. Jesus says no, and charges the church with culpability in tolerating this situation.

We in 21st-century Britain live in a post-Christian, secular, humanist culture, where we are pressured to accept habits and activities which go against Christ's teachings. The pressure is more than social ostracisation; it is sometimes enshrined in law. Many face stark choices, where careers and relationships are threatened.

The church is the body of Christ on earth. He who was without sin cannot have a body which tolerates it. It is not enough for a church to have active programmes of global outreach, service in the local community and pastoral care of its congregation. The Rotary Club does that. What distinguishes the church is purity, which is only possible when believers walk close to Jesus.

But purity is a brutal master and is not the bottom line. Love is. God's pure heart beats with love. We are called to love the Lord with everything we have, and our neighbour as ourselves. How do we know what compromise shows love and what compromise reveals a capitulation to sin?

And if we can figure that out, we may find there is a price to pay: financial, personal or career- or church-related. Are we willing to pay it?

Lord, where have I compromised in my own life? Where do I see my church compromising on important principles? Where has love hardened into brittle judgementalism? Help!

MICHELE D. MORRISON

Wake up!

'**I know your deeds; you have a reputation of being alive, but you are dead. Wake up! Strengthen what remains and is about to die, for I have found your deeds unfinished in the sight of my God.**' (NIV)

I am writing this in January 2021, when Covid-19 continues to ravage the world. Recently we purchased a small device which instantly reads the level of oxygen in the blood, because we heard that hospitals are receiving Covid patients who appear fairly strong, but when medics take a reading of oxygen levels, they recognise immediately that a patient is beyond recovery. It is too late to save a life which is so low in oxygen. If the patient had seen the drop in oxygenation earlier, she could have presented sooner, when recovery was still possible.

This letter is like an oxygen meter to the church in Sardis. 'You think your outward appearance reflects an inner spiritual health,' Jesus says, 'but in fact, you're breathing yesterday's air; you're trading in past glory; your love and faith are waning, and your service and perseverance are a thing of the past. Wake up now, or it will be too late!'

Jesus exhorts this outwardly flourishing, inwardly dying church to shake itself and strengthen what little life remains. Having a good reputation in the eyes of the world can sometimes take priority over inner wholeness and ethical integrity. These words are hard-hitting. There are no pats on the back. The situation is dire.

This sobering letter should challenge us to take a good, hard look at our church and our individual faith. We are in the age of mega-churches, and smaller congregations can feel that they are in their shadow. But a large building filled with enthusiastic worshippers is not the mark of spiritual life, Jesus warns. It's the steady walk with Jesus that counts, the eloquence of deeds that he hears, and the lives of service, of compassion and kindness and of faith that he sees.

If your church resembles the one in Sardis, be challenged to keep your own 'clothes' clean and to keep your own faith alive, so that Jesus will not erase your name from the book of life.

MICHELE D. MORRISON

Fake news from the fake Jews

'I know that you have little strength, yet you have kept my word and have not denied my name.' (NIV)

The beleaguered church in Philadelphia gets no correction from the Lord. Persecuted and suffering, the church has remained faithful despite the temptations and taunts of the fake Jews.

The tenderness of the good shepherd is seen clearly in his words to those who have kept his word and not denied his name. He who holds the key of David has opened the door no one can shut, and that open door yawns before them. Sharing one's faith does not require money and strength, a great planning strategy and charismatic leaders; it just needs humble people who love Jesus and who recognise their own weakness to the extent that they put their full trust in the Lord.

During World War II, my mother joined the US Marines. Raised on a farm in Wisconsin, she had a strong faith and resisted the ridicule of the more worldly women she met in boot camp. Now, at the age of 96 and residing in a care home half a world away from me, she is isolated in her room during Covid lockdowns. Her confused mind has forgotten many things, but she has not forgotten her love for her Saviour. When staff at the home enable a Skype call with me, the care worker who holds the iPad for Mom overhears a conversation liberally salted with faith in the God who never fails. One woman remarked how much love she'd witnessed during our call and how encouraged she felt. Mom may have little strength, but she has kept Jesus' word and has not denied his name.

Jesus is fully involved in every aspect of salvation. 'I will make… I will keep… I will write… I will do it.' Jesus will do it. He promises never to leave nor forsake us.

Thank you, Lord, that my impact for the sake of the gospel does not depend on my strength but rather on my weakness. Blessed are the poor in spirit, for theirs is the kingdom of heaven. Amen

MICHELE D. MORRISON

Guess who's coming to dinner?

'Here I am! I stand at the door and knock. If anyone hears my voice and opens the door, I will come in and eat with that person, and they with me.' (NIV)

This letter is rich with vivid images. We often hear the phrase, 'because you are lukewarm – neither hot nor cold – I am about to spit you out of my mouth' (v. 16). The Laodicean water supply carried calciferous water across a sun-drenched aqueduct into the city – by the time citizens received it, it was tepid and foul. The church would have had no trouble understanding Jesus' meaning; being likened to a disgusting taste must have been shocking. Jesus' strong declaration that he was going to vomit them out must have been shaming.

Shock tactics are often employed for a reason. Jesus doesn't want the Laodiceans to be dazzled by cheap gold and miss the real thing, which only he can give. His present is his presence at our tables. He doesn't want us to miss his knock at the door of our hearts.

When I was a child, family dinners could be fairly lengthy affairs as we lingered over the food, sharing details of our day, ideas we'd been considering and activities we were engaged in. They were a time when relationships deepened. They could be precious and memorable. Not every mealtime was so rich, of course. We were busy with schoolwork and meetings; sometimes dinners were rushed affairs and sometimes there were angry words. That only made the leisurely meals more precious.

Customs have changed; many people eat in virtual isolation in front of a screen or lead busy lives which allow little time for gracious dining. Sometimes mealtimes can be fraught, as children resist eating the food they're given, manners need refining and tempers fray.

I believe Jesus offers a mealtime where he lingers with us, gently guiding our understanding to realign our perceptions. No special menu is required, because the quality of relationship will always trump the quality of the food.

If your faith has grown lukewarm, and you suspect that your apparent wealth masks actual poverty, give your blurred eyes a chance to clear as you listen for, open your heart to and sit down with Jesus.

MICHELE D. MORRISON

Questions Jesus asked

Rachel Ridler writes:

My husband (who does a lot of lecturing) often responds to his students' questions by asking them a question. I am sure his students must get frustrated when he does not answer their queries straightaway, when all they want is to be able to write down the answer.

Sometimes when mentoring or counselling people in my small groups, I have used similar tactics. It's a way of trying to get to the root of the problem, the reason why someone is asking the question. This might sound familiar to you, or maybe not. But it probably won't surprise you that we're not the first people in history to do this. In fact, Jesus could often be found asking a question in response to a question and using questions carefully to find out the reason behind what others were doing or asking him.

In this series we are going to be looking in more detail at the questions that Jesus asked. What did he ask? When did he ask them? Why did he ask them? What purpose do the questions Jesus asked that are recorded in the Bible serve? Is there a pattern or a theme to his questions?

Essentially, being a Christian is a decision, the answer to a very important question – will you accept Jesus into your life as your Lord and Saviour? Leading up to that are lots of other questions that we need to ponder and contemplate about ourselves, God and our own lives. It makes complete sense that Jesus would use questions to make his audiences think, rather than being spoon-fed with answers that they don't really understand.

As I have spent time reading through the four gospels and choosing which questions to study, I have realised how very many questions Jesus did ask. The 14 we will be looking at in more detail over the next two weeks are just the tip of the iceberg. Let's pray as we begin:

Father God, please open our hearts to the questions that Jesus asks throughout the gospel accounts. Help us to examine ourselves, help us to ponder together and help us to draw our own conclusions on the questions ahead. Thank you that you gave us minds so that we can think for ourselves and that you don't force us to love and accept you. Amen

Questions of a young boy

'Why were you searching for me?' he asked. 'Didn't you know I had to be in my Father's house?' But they did not understand what he was saying to them. (NIV)

Nothing can beat the innocence of youth. The questions asked by children are the sweetest, funniest and most sincere. Unfiltered and curious, never sensing the undertone of the conversation, they just go straight ahead and ask what they want!

I can sense that here in Jesus' question. He doesn't hear the underlying panic in his parents' voice as they rush back to find him, thinking the worst. He does not seem to understand the error of his actions or why his parents would even be concerned. To him, he was safe and well, in the exact right place that he should be. He wasn't lost or missing; he was sitting in the presence of his Father.

I can fully step into his parents' shoes and understand the absolute fear and panic that sets in when you can't find your child. When you find them, relief and anger combine as you try to make them understand the gravity of the situation and why they should not wander off again. If I were in that hyper-emotional state, I'm sure I too would have missed the point of what Jesus was saying.

'Didn't you know I had to be in my Father's house?' He was drawn to connect with his heavenly Father in that moment, and that was all that mattered. As much as I'm sure he loved his earthly parents, Jesus knew he had a connection to something greater. Perhaps in those early years, when Jesus was a baby and toddler, doing and learning in the same way as every other young child, his parents had forgotten his miraculous conception and birth. They missed who he was, and not even his innocent childlike question could remind them.

What part of Jesus' story or identity are you missing? Spend a few moments asking God to reveal the things that you have missed in the busyness of life and in having lost our childlike thoughts.

RACHEL RIDLER

A 'whodunnit' question

At once Jesus realised that power had gone out from him. He turned round in the crowd and asked, 'Who touched my clothes?' 'You see the people crowding against you,' his disciples answered, 'and yet you can ask, "Who touched me?"' But Jesus kept looking around to see who had done it. (NIV)

A box of chocolates arrives in the post, but there is no note to say who sent it and I don't recognise the writing on the address label. While I am over the moon for this unexpected gift, I am left wondering how I can possibly thank the sender. As much as I try, it remains a mystery.

The situation is different here, but the same question of 'whodunnit' applies. Jesus is walking through a crowded place and feels someone touch him – someone with faith, who receives healing from that action. Knowing what has happened, there seems to be an urgency in Jesus' question here: 'Who touched my clothes?' He needs to know so that he can follow up on that action. He has something he wants to say to them or to do with them, but he is unable to locate them.

The disciples seem unaware of the importance of this, and obviously feel that it is an impossible task to find the person, given the number of people surrounding them. Just as I gave up on trying to find out who my mystery chocolate-sender was, the disciples seem quite happy to move on. But Jesus is not willing to do that. You see, when Jesus finds someone with that little bit of faith, he wants to encourage them. He wants to see that faith grow and flourish, and he wants them to know what a difference their faith in him has made.

What happens when the healed woman comes forward? Jesus tells her that her faith has healed her and that she can finally be restored to her family and community. Those words added meaning to her healing, and were worth Jesus pursuing the question of 'whodunnit'.

Lord Jesus, thank you for your faithfulness in pursuing us and encouraging us in our faith. Help us to keep searching for answers to our difficult questions, and to love and pursue others so that they may know you too. Amen

RACHEL RIDLER

A question of perspective

'Why do you see the speck that is in your brother's eye, but do not notice the log that is in your own eye? Or how can you say to your brother, "Let me take the speck out of your eye", when there is the log in your own eye?' (ESV)

Here in Britain, we love a good old moan! We love to point out everyone else's flaws, while being blissfully unaware of our own. This might seem harmless over a good cup of tea with a friend, but we have seen how destructive this can be in the media. In fact, it can be so hurtful that it pushes people to quit careers they love, to experience severe mental health or even to commit suicide.

So what does Jesus say about the matter? Interestingly, here in the sermon on the mount, he does not tell us to point out the flaws of those around us. Instead, he has a question for us all to ponder in our own hearts – why? He wants us to ask ourselves why we do this. Why do we think it's okay? Why do we not see our own flaws and deal with them? Why do we feel the need to point out other people's flaws? Why is this a problem?

The key issue here is not what each of our flaws is, or whose is the biggest and worst. It is a question of perspective, not one of comparison. Perspective is different. It asks us to consider where we are coming from, what our view is. It forces us to change the way we do things. And Jesus challenges us to deal with our own issues first and everyone else's second. By doing this, perhaps our hearts will change as we do this and we will not feel the need to spot other's problems. Instead, we will just walk alongside and help them as we both grow and deal with things together.

Lord Jesus, please help me to recognise my own flaws first so that together we can deal with them. Please help me to love others by changing my perspective and walking alongside them. Amen

RACHEL RIDLER

A question of faith

'Why are you so frightened?' Jesus answered. 'What little faith you have!' Then he got up and ordered the winds and the waves to stop, and there was a great calm. (GNT)

Once again Jesus hits us with a question that has a very obvious answer! 'Why are you so frightened?' should not be a necessary question when you are stuck on a boat in the middle of a storm. I almost want to yell back at him, 'Because we might die on this boat in the storm!' I imagine the disciples having a similar reaction and perhaps just pointing at the waves in an animated fashion with a look of disbelief on their faces.

And yet Jesus does not give the response we expect. He shows the disciples that actually there is nothing to be worried or frightened about. He is on the boat with them, he has the power to calm the storm and, even if he didn't, death is not to be feared anymore.

I often think of this verse when life gets on top of me, and I feel a storm brewing (either real or metaphorical). My natural reaction can often be to panic, to try to fix things and to find a solution to the problem myself. But in those times, I try to read this verse and remind myself of the importance of the words.

First, I have God on my side, and if I have faith in him then he *can* calm the storm. He has the power and authority to change circumstances, to break chains and to bring freedom. Have I asked him?

Second, he is there with me. No matter what I'm going through, he is always by my side, holding me and carrying me through. The storm may go on longer than I want it to, but he is always in the midst of life's ups and downs with me, and I know that he will never leave my side.

Father, I thank you that you are powerful enough to calm my storms. I ask you to calm the storms that I am going through right now and to help me see that there is nothing to be frightened of when you are by my side. Amen
RACHEL RIDLER

A question of motives

He said to them, 'If any of you has a sheep and it falls into a pit on the Sabbath, will you not take hold of it and lift it out? How much more valuable is a person than a sheep! Therefore it is lawful to do good on the Sabbath.' (NIV)

There are many instances in the Bible when we see people come to Jesus with intentions to trap him and catch him out. This verse comes after Jesus has been asked if it is lawful to heal (in this case, a man's hand). The Pharisees were trying to find a way to 'bring charges against Jesus' (v. 10), and they immediately spotted an opportunity. Even the most uneducated Jews at the time would have known the ten commandments and the command to 'remember the Sabbath day by keeping it holy' (Exodus 20:8). This meant that one day was for rest from all kinds of work.

What Jesus is really putting under the microscope and questioning with his reply are the motivations of the Pharisees and the real purpose behind the fourth commandment. The Pharisees have latched on to the word 'work' and made sure that anything even remotely related to work is against the rules. They have taken the commandments to the extreme, intent on raising themselves up and making others feel inferior when they struggle to keep the fine details of the law.

Jesus tries to remind them that at the heart of the law is community. It was there to show them how to live well together and how to love God. Yes, their bodies and minds need rest, and time needs to be dedicated to God. But this was not meant to be at the expense of community and loving others.

Moreover, the sabbath was created for our good (Mark 2:27). It was never meant to be a burden.

What things do you make extra rules about in your life or try to enforce on those around you? Ask God to remind you about the heart of his law – to do good and to love and value those around you just like he does.

RACHEL RIDLER

A question of identity

When Jesus came to the region of Caesarea Philippi, he asked his disciples, 'Who do people say the Son of Man is?' They replied, 'Some say John the Baptist; others say Elijah; and still others, Jeremiah or one of the prophets.' 'But what about you?' he asked. 'Who do you say I am?' (NIV)

Identity is important. But our concept of it now is very different to what it was in Jesus' time. Our culture encourages us to stand out as an individual, to be unique and valued for our attributes or life decisions. When asked who we are, we might talk about our jobs, our achievements, our hobbies, our sexual orientation or our gender.

But in Jesus' day, your identity came through your relationships, your bloodline and your tribe. Who you were connected to was of utmost importance, and here Jesus wants to know who his disciples think he is. Jesus never went about proclaiming his identity. In fact, there are many instances where he asks people not to tell anyone who he really is. Instead, he wants people to come to an understanding on their own.

In many ways he embodies the saying 'Actions speak louder than words.' Jesus could very well have announced that he was the Son of God wherever he went, but instead he allowed his teaching, his love and care for people, his miracles and his link to God to shine out from him, showing people who he really was through his actions.

The disciples list a few significant and influential people from the past as possible identities for Jesus. It would be a huge compliment to be connected to any one of them. But here is the key question – and the one for all of us to contemplate: 'Who do you say I am?' It does not matter what others think or how many of Jesus' individual attributes or achievements we recognise. All that matters is who we say Jesus is – who is he connected to? Is he God's Son or not?

Spend some time with this question of who Jesus is. Is he God's Son or not, and why do you believe that? Pray that, like Jesus, our identities as children of God and our link to God would shine out through our actions.

RACHEL RIDLER

A question of love

'What do you think? If a man owns a hundred sheep, and one of them wanders away, will he not leave the ninety-nine on the hills and go to look for the one that wandered off?' (NIV)

What is the most valuable thing that you've ever lost? Maybe it was your keys, your phone or your bank card (the key to all your hard-earned money). I remember getting so worked up about losing my phone a few years ago. I had purposely bought one that was bright orange so that I would never lose it, and yet when I returned home from a shopping trip, I couldn't find it.

Panicked, I sent my husband back to the supermarket to look under every shelf and down every aisle, while I checked the car and the house and rang my number to see if we could hear the phone vibrating. We could not find it anywhere and so I called to cancel it and order a new one (easier to do with phones than sheep). The next day I went to load up the washing machine and out fell a bright orange phone! Perhaps not the rejoicing moment that it would have been the day before…

I love how Jesus starts this story with a question: 'What do you think?' Before he even tells his story, he is asking those gathered to put on their thinking caps and ponder with him. He is not going to tell them the right answer; he wants them to deliberate with him.

We are seeing the true value of Jesus' questions now. He doesn't want to force people to come to a conclusion but wants to allow them the space to think and decide themselves. In this verse, he is questioning our love for others and our understanding of God's love for us. Do we think we are worth chasing down when we wander off? Do we think others are worth finding too? Or are we content with the people who are already saved and who already know Jesus?

How much do you love people who don't know Jesus yet? Would you be willing to pursue them with as much energy as you would a lost phone, key or bank card? Pray and ask God to develop that love in you for the lost.

RACHEL RIDLER

Questioning the order

'But you are not to be like that. Instead, the greatest among you should be like the youngest, and the one who rules like the one who serves. For who is greater, the one who is at the table or the one who serves? Is it not the one who is at the table? But I am among you as one who serves.' (NIV)

I remember when I first went to university. I was a naive 18-year-old with all my mother's hand-me-down wisdom in my head. The meals we usually ate and the way we did things at home had seemed normal, and I hadn't ever considered that there might be other ways to do things. This became apparent one Sunday morning. Without access to an ironing board, I had taken to doing my ironing on the floor of our corridor in the relative peace and quiet before heading off to church. As I minded my own business, a hungover flatmate appeared and shattered my world by simply asking why I was ironing all my underwear. It had never occurred to me to question this activity, as my mum had always done it. Thus ended the period in my life when I ironed my underwear!

Sometimes a simple question can shatter everything you have ever thought was true. In this verse, Jesus turns the accepted social order on its head: 'Who is greater, the one who sits and eats or the one who serves?' As the disciples bicker after dinner about who will be greatest, each wanting to beat the other, Jesus takes the opportunity to teach them an important lesson. In the kingdom of God, it is those who serve who will be the greatest, and those who think of themselves as important will be the least. Jesus then offers himself as a living, breathing example of this by serving them all in many ways, even by washing their feet, the lowest job of all. I wonder if the disciples shared a moment of stunned silence as this news sunk in. If they carried on acting as they did, fighting over who is greatest, none of them would be.

What do you value in this world? What makes you feel great and how will you measure your success in life? Spend some time today pondering if Jesus would think they are important too and aligning your values with his.

RACHEL RIDLER

Technical questions

Jesus knew right away what they were thinking, and said, 'Why are you so sceptical? Which is simpler: to say to the paraplegic, "I forgive your sins," or say, "Get up, take your stretcher, and start walking"?' (MSG)

I have a confession to make: I've never really understood this question that Jesus posed. As a child, all I could think when I heard it was that 'I forgive your sins' was a much shorter sentence than the other, so surely that made it easier to say! Like the crowd surrounding him, I didn't get the point Jesus was trying to make.

This is a question of technicalities and of proving what you can do. Maybe as a child you got into a bragging competition – one where you claimed that you could score more goals than someone else or eat more chocolate than them. All these claims are hypothetical unless you have something to back it up – a 'Highest Scorer of the Season' certificate from your football club or a chocolate-eating competition medal. But nothing really proves something as much as seeing it with your own eyes.

In his university days, my husband was challenged to drink a whole vat of chocolate fondue. He had been bold enough to claim he could, but when he got the cup of molten chocolate to his lips and took the first gulp, he cried out in pain. He hadn't factored in that molten chocolate would be hot! He couldn't back up his claim.

What Jesus is really asking here is whether the crowd believes he can do something that cannot be proved in the physical realm. He can't bring out a certificate that says 'Son of God' or do something visible to show that their sins are forgiven. But he can prove he has power to heal, and they saw that with their own eyes. I guess it is then up to them to decide if he is telling the truth about the other statement too.

Father, help me to believe you when I can't see proof with my own eyes. Help me to trust Jesus' identity and power as the Son of God and to put my life into his hands, even when others might think it is foolish. Amen

RACHEL RIDLER

Questioning our way of life

'Who of you by worrying can add a single hour to your life? Since you cannot do this very little thing, why do you worry about the rest?' (NIV)

When I was a teenager, I wanted to encourage my parents, who were struggling. My dad had hurt his back and was signed off sick from work. His employer had reacted unsympathetically and, assuming he was interviewing for other jobs, called a tribunal against him. It was the most stressed I had seen my parents in my short life, and I felt helpless. I wanted to show them love and comfort, but I didn't know how. I had just discovered this verse, so I wrote it on a Post-It note and left it on my dad's bedside table. I'm not sure if it brought them much comfort at the time, but I hope it made them question things.

Jesus asks this crucial question to all of us: why do you worry? It is a question of where our hearts lie, what we truly believe and if we are willing to really live out what we say we believe. If we have understood who Jesus is – the power that he has to forgive and heal, how much he loves us and that he is someone we can trust – then worry should not even enter our minds. All those things that we are stressing over, God can heal or change if we ask him to. All those things that bother us, we can bring to God and receive his comfort and love. All those things that are too big to handle, we can trust God to take from us and deal with.

This question is a reality check for us all. Are we *actually* willing to live differently, trusting God with everything and seeking his will? If we are, then worry doesn't need to be in our lives anymore.

Dear Father God, I want to live differently, trusting in you and your power in my life. Please help me to put off worry and instead to give the cares of this life over to you. Amen

RACHEL RIDLER

A question of memory

Jesus (overhearing them): Why are you focusing on bread? Don't you see yet? Don't you understand? You have eyes – why don't you see? You have ears – why don't you hear? Are you so hard-hearted? Don't you remember when I broke the five rounds of flatbread among the 5,000? Tell Me, how many baskets of scraps were left over? **Disciples:** Twelve.
(VOICE)

Can you picture this scene? The disciples (who have been around Jesus for some time now) completely misinterpret what he is saying to them. They're in the boat, hungry because they don't have enough food, while Jesus teaches a lesson about the Pharisees. He warns them to place their trust and faith in him, rather than constantly demand proof. And, as they often do, they get confused.

I wonder if Jesus is disappointed in them in this moment. After the conversations they've had and the things they've seen, the disciples still don't truly grasp what Jesus is saying to them, who he is or what his kingdom is like. His final question to them is one of desperation, trying to jog their memories and help them out. It's like he's giving them the clue to the answer to his question, but they still don't get it. They answer 'twelve' because they are focused on their needs for food.

Maybe you're scoffing at them and thinking that you're never like that; that you always seek to understand scripture and never forget what Jesus did. But how long does your spiritual memory last? When you face challenges, do you immediately remind yourself of all the things God has done in the past? You may think that the time God provided a job interview is unrelated to your family member's health issues right now, but God is providing for you through them both. God is good and powerful, and his goodness doesn't change. We just need to keep our focus on him.

Make a list of all the amazing ways in which God has worked in your life in the past. Put it somewhere visible so that it daily jogs your memory when new issues and challenges come up.

RACHEL RIDLER

A trick question

Jesus, however, was aware of their evil plan, and so he said, 'You hypocrites! Why are you trying to trap me? Show me the coin for paying the tax!' They brought him the coin, and he asked them, 'Whose face and name are these?' (GNT)

I vividly remember the day my boss at my first full-time job slammed a bottle of wine down on the conference room table next to me. She knew that I was a Christian and that I had chosen not to drink, partly because of my religious beliefs. The bottle of wine was both a challenge and a trap. At the end of the team meeting, she dismissed everyone except me, asking what my reaction to the bottle of wine was. I knew there was no right answer and that, in the same way the Pharisees ask Jesus a trick question about taxes in this passage, whatever I said would be used against me.

Jesus, however, is wise to the Pharisees' plans. He senses their motives and answers their question with another: 'Whose face is on the coin?' He chooses not to fall into the trap, but to play their own game, giving them pause for thought. He asks them also to consider their motives and ask themselves why they feel the need to ask trick questions.

Perhaps we have done the same with God in the past: given him ultimatums or questions where neither answer will actually make us want to trust him. God declines to answer. Instead, he asks us a question: 'What are your motives? Why is your heart doing this?'

When I considered my boss' motives for trying to trap me, I think it was because she saw something in my rock-solid faith that challenged her to consider her own beliefs. When she struggled with that, she decided to attack me instead. Let's not attack God because we are scared, but instead dig into our hearts and find out what is really going on.

Consider your heart today. Are you trying to trap God or catch him out? Be vulnerable and open with God about what scares you about having faith in him and ask him to help you to trust him.

RACHEL RIDLER

A rhetorical question?

At three o'clock Jesus cried out with a loud shout, '*Eloi, Eloi, lema sabachthani*?' which means, 'My God, my God, why did you abandon me?' (GNT)

As we reach the end of Jesus' life on earth, his questions become more serious and perhaps more rhetorical. A rhetorical question is one asked in order to create a dramatic effect or to make a point rather than to get an answer. Not that I think Jesus was trying to create drama (the Pharisees did that all by themselves), but I do think that his final question before dying was not one with a particular answer, but one that makes a point to us all.

Jesus *knew* his mission here on earth would end with crucifixion. The night before he was betrayed, he wept in the garden of Gethsemane, pleading for God to take away what was coming, but also knowing the implications of it and that he needed to go through with it. Jesus isn't crying out here for an explanation from God as to why he is on the cross and all alone, but rather making a point that we all need to consider personally.

Like all the other questions we have considered in this study, his final question is for the benefit of those around him and for us too. This question cuts us to the heart and forces us to consider uncomfortable things about ourselves. Why did we do the things that sent Jesus to the cross? What are we going to do about this man who gave his life for us? How do we react to the pain and anguish he went through on our behalf?

God abandoned his own Son so that he could be with you. What could be a more powerful message of love than that? I guess if it was for dramatic effect, then the cliffhanger is this – God is waiting for your answer to his proposal. Will you love him back?

Take some time today to truly consider what Jesus went through on the cross for you and the love that he showed. Respond to God and this extravagant show of love in your own way.

RACHEL RIDLER

A joyful question

He asked her, 'Woman, why are you crying? Who is it you are looking for?' Thinking he was the gardener, she said, 'Sir, if you have carried him away, tell me where you have put him, and I will get him.' (NIV)

You might think 'a joyful question' is a curious title when the passage begins with someone weeping. Is Jesus toying with Mary when he asks such an obvious question? He clearly knows who she is. He knows the events of the last few days, and he knows exactly why she is crying. These are not questions that Jesus needs the answer to, but ones he needs Mary to consider.

Mary is blind to something right in front of her. It's like the many times that I get confused when I am talking to someone on my mobile phone, while also searching for said phone because I need to add a date into my calendar! I am blind to the fact that the phone is right there in my hand, and I need someone to come and ask me, 'Who are you talking to on the phone?', to make me realise where the phone is.

Jesus could have said straight away, 'Stop crying, Mary. It's me, Jesus!' But like he has before, he is allowing her space to discover who he is for herself.

As much as we would love for God to come and demonstrate the truth of who he is by performing miracles for each of us, God knows it wouldn't make a difference. Faith and understanding grow from gentle revelation, questioning and a gradual realisation of who God is and how much he loves us.

So, this *is* a joyful question for Jesus to finish on. It is the one that triggers Mary's revelation of who he is and the joy of resurrection life for both her and us.

Who or what is it that you are looking for in life? Have Jesus' questions forced you to consider your viewpoint on him and God's love for you?

RACHEL RIDLER

How to deal with doubt

Victoria Byrne writes:

If there were no room for doubt, there would be no room for choice – or for faith. It's our privilege to refuse to doubt and to choose to trust Jesus every day. 'To whom shall we go?' asks Peter. 'You have the words of eternal life' (John 6:68, NIV). Peter's words reassure me of my allegiance, too. They stop me worrying about the minutiae of my faith journey, or how well I'm following Jesus. Peter's rhetorical question prompts me to turn to Jesus and reaffirm: 'I'll go with you; you have the words of life.' We also have Paul's assurance that nothing can separate us from the love of God (Romans 8:38–39).

In heaven, we will be able to see God with clarity, unobstructed by our fears, sins, misunderstandings and preferences. Until we get there, we are in a unique phase of our existence, when this possibility for doubt offers an opportunity to honour God with our freely given trust. Right now we can each take daily steps to notice God's goodness and believe that he wants to connect more closely with us. Otherwise we can believe the accuser and invest in what separates us from God. When we choose to draw closer to God, it delights the heart of the one who loves us. To deal with doubt is to handle as best we can the various challenges we face until that day comes.

Doubt is a natural part of our daily experience, and it doesn't always mean doubting God. So much of the struggle is when we doubt ourselves, or others around us. That's when we can feel undermined. But be encouraged that it's God who is the Father in this relationship: he is the one in charge of leading the way.

In the end it comes down to simply stated truths: God is good, so we follow him as best we can. Growing in that trust is a life's work. Scripture was written to help us, so I hope these two weeks will encourage you on your way. Know that you have the Holy Spirit to help you as you read and as you put into practice whatever he reveals to you. God is faithful; one day you and I will discover how much he was doing behind the scenes.

What does God think of our doubts?

Still unconvinced, Thomas replied, 'There's no way I'm going to believe this unless I personally see the wounds of the nails in his hands, touch them with my finger, and put my hand into the wound of his side where he was pierced!' (TPT)

When I'm dealing with a doubt, I'm rarely aware that my faith is being challenged. Since coming to faith, whenever I've read the gospels, I don't think I've ever said, 'I just don't believe that happened.' My doubts tend to lurk unnoticed.

Thomas isn't like me. When he heard from his fellow disciples that Jesus had shown up and proven he was still alive, Thomas effectively said, 'I'll believe that when I see it.' Thomas declared that unless he could put his hand in the wound in Jesus' body, he would remain unconvinced. This is a pretty extreme ultimatum. It's gross and sounds presumptuous; touching the wound is the opposite of keeping reverent distance from a rabbi (or God!) whom you respect. Thomas sounds hurt and angry. Maybe there is more to his doubt than simple unbelief. Had he been disappointed or traumatised by those events of the crucifixion and all the turmoil? Was it too painful for Thomas to dare hope that Jesus had returned?

Next time I fear God could be offended by my doubts, I'm going to remind myself of Jesus' reaction when he meets Thomas. Jesus miraculously enters the room, knows Thomas' sceptical, defensive thoughts and takes him at his word. He does not push him away, he invites him closer, willing to help his faith. He meets Thomas' needs readily. I have heard of people in moments of crisis praying, 'God, if you're real, please help,' and God answers their deepest need. He is willing to answer the prayers of those who have great doubts.

Do I fear I should have all the answers because I've been a believer for a long time? God is less offended by my doubt than I am. I could just ask God to show me more.

What emotions have been involved when you have wrestled with a doubt?

VICTORIA BYRNE

Using scripture to strengthen our faith

Jesus performed many other signs in the presence of his disciples, which are not recorded in this book. But these are written that you may believe that Jesus is the Messiah, the Son of God, and that by believing you may have life in his name. (NIV)

It's important to engage with our doubts as we read the Bible. If we bury them, they may grow. For example, we read of Jesus' miracles, but we may nurse a doubt that says, 'I've never seen God work a miracle in my life.' That belief could so easily become, 'God doesn't care about me' or 'God can't answer my prayers.' What if we acknowledged and challenged these doubts about the miraculous? How often have you reviewed your prayers and noticed how the answers just 'fell into place'? Maybe you bumped into the exact person you needed to contact. When I notice even the small answers to prayer, I am aware of the signs of God's presence.

Right after yesterday's passage in John's gospel, John states that he wrote it to build our faith (v. 31). This is why it's helpful to get a regular diet of scripture; the Bible describes other people's interactions with God, and they help us have our own interactions with him. Reading how he intervenes for others helps us keep alert for him in the present.

With this in mind we can read the Bible as a book of possibilities and believe that God is ready to work in our lives in ways that mirror what he has done through other people. Jesus even said we 'will do even greater things' than he did (John 14:12–14). If we do not challenge our doubts, we lower our sights. We might miss what God wants to do. He wants to partner with our faith. That's why the gospel writers wanted to strengthen our confidence in God. They describe God's reality, what his kingdom is like and all its possibilities. God's word helps whatever your circumstance. God's love for his people shines through every page.

Father God, thank you for answering my prayers, even when I haven't noticed. The Bible says, 'You do not have because you do not ask' (James 4:2), so I ask: please strengthen my faith. Amen

VICTORIA BYRNE

God was with me there!

When Jacob awoke from his sleep, he thought, 'Surely the Lord is in this place, and I was not aware of it.' He was afraid and said, 'How awesome is this place! This is none other than the house of God; this is the gate of heaven.' (NIV)

Yesterday a friend asked me to pray with her. I was reminded of a passage from Numbers which wouldn't go away. In hindsight, I'm surprised how many excuses I came up with to doubt that this idea was from God – 'It's just my train of thought' (it wasn't), 'It has an obvious connection with her situation' (not really)… on and on. After she shared how this relevant passage had helped her, I saw how unfounded my fears were.

How much I doubt God's ability to give me answers to in-the-moment problems! One valuable tool for coaching myself in how God 'speaks' is a journal. As I write, I realise how stuck I am and how much I need God's wisdom; so I write what I think I've heard from him, in the spirit of having a go. Sometimes I just write further reflections of my own. Having put it on paper, I can review it – perhaps days or months later. I mark the page, perhaps add a word in the margin, so I can have fun finding these nuggets later and seeing where God was moving. It helps me recognise him next time.

It always amazes me how it wasn't obvious at the time that it was God, but later the volume seems turned up to maximum! They are often his loving response to whatever I've been venting. Sometimes I've written, 'I wonder if…?' and my later self responds, 'Of course!' The signs are there: the words shout of his reassurance, perhaps specific events or actions which later happened or helped.

I identify with Jacob. We wrestle with our thoughts, but when we wake up, we have a different viewpoint. We can take the lesson into the new day, that God is with us, even when we don't always realise it at the time.

What did God say to you yesterday?

VICTORIA BYRNE

How truth encourages us

Samaritans from that town believed in him because of the woman's testimony, 'He told me everything I've ever done.' So when the Samaritans came to him, they urged him to stay with them, and he stayed two days. And because of his words many more became believers. (NIV)

Last night I attended an online worship and prayer evening. We had a chance to bless each other by quietly praying and listening for encouraging words that God wanted us to share with another individual in our group, and we each took turns. We were doing what the Samaritan woman was doing – having a conversation with God – and giving him a chance to give people individually tailored words of encouragement. Most of the time we gave things that seemed like obvious truths, about hope, love or their character, but in every case, it meant more to the person receiving than it did to the person giving. This felt to me like a small sign that it was from God: he knows what we need to hear more than others might imagine.

One friend spoke beautiful things over me that helped me see myself through God's loving eyes. I've been pondering the way that this caused me to focus more fully on God, rather than on myself.

Today's passage reminds me that when we connect with God and he tells us about ourselves, it leads to us worshipping him (not ourselves). I find it hugely helpful to my levels of faith, when other Christians listen out for what God has to say to me. It is one way God overcomes doubt, being vividly present to us.

The Holy Spirit helps us to more clearly see the character of God, as Jesus did for this woman in Samaria. She had certain expectations of how a rabbi should behave, for example, avoiding contact with Samaritans and women. Jesus surprised her in revealing more about her life, but also more about himself. He helped her dismiss her doubts and turn her gaze to Jesus.

How could a practice of listening to God help your levels of faith?

VICTORIA BYRNE

Pulling up weeds

Commit to the Lord whatever you do, and he will establish your plans. The Lord works out everything to its proper end. (NIV)

I used to be a terror for second-guessing myself. Nowadays I'm recovering from my addiction to indecision. I'm learning to encourage myself to press ahead by (prayerfully) making my default plan 'The Plan'.

Doubts can so easily creep in if we're not frequently turning to God. When trying to tackle a tricky task, I'd wonder if I should even be doing it this way. As I peacefully cut the hedge in my front garden by hand, enjoying the thinking space, doubts would creep in that I ought to be doing it more efficiently, especially when kind neighbours pass by offering me their electric hedge trimmers. But I enjoy the slow pace. I always have a fruitful time pondering things while I'm cutting the hedge. And there's no danger of cutting through the power cable! Which power source is more important: God and this opportunity to think and pray, or electricity to shred the little twigs as quickly as possible?

These self-doubts are actually doubts about God's loving care, as well as my own envious insecurities. I'm looking at other people's lives and thinking their lifestyle, their career, their gifts would be better for me than my own. I realise it's a crazy way to think when I remember that God cares for us (1 Peter 5:7); he prepares works in advance for us to do (Ephesians 2:10; Jeremiah 29:11); and even equips us to do them (Hebrews 13:20–21). Love does not envy.

Paul reminds us to run 'the race marked out for us' (Hebrews 12:1), giving us the image of a track athlete who needs to stay in their lane, not run someone else's race, as we make a beeline for God's destination.

'Trust in the Lord with all your heart and lean not on your own understanding; in all your ways submit to him, and he will make your paths straight' (Proverbs 3:5–6).

VICTORIA BYRNE

Nurture self-doubts or welcome God?

'Pardon me, my lord,' Gideon replied, 'but how can I save Israel? My clan is the weakest in Manasseh, and I am the least in my family.' The Lord answered, 'I will be with you.' (NIV)

I used to be very shy, so I understand how Gideon might imagine that a cramped winepress would be a good place to thresh his wheat, because at least he could hide. He hides because there are marauding armies about and Gideon feels weak and vulnerable to attack. He is focused on the risk to his precious crop – on what he has to lose – and has not considered what he might do to avert the threat.

So he is hiding, but even then he does not feel safe; he feels 'abandoned' by God. When God does speak to him, he is not excited at the thought of rescuing his people, because he feels unqualified, under-resourced and fearful of the people he is supposed to bless.

I recall some particularly dire outings in my younger days when I was silent and unhappy for the whole event, focused on thinking I had nothing valuable to say. I know now that I would have benefited from understanding how God saw me. Even in adulthood, I have often felt inadequate to professional challenges, while others disagreed and tried to reassure me. One summer God persistently showed me his perception of me and of my work. One day he said: 'I am the one who is calling you a leader, so you can call yourself a leader.' I've been significantly more confident and at peace since then.

Gideon sees himself through God's eyes for the first time. Where he considered himself the least of his people, God sees him as a mighty warrior who will save his entire people (not even just his clan). This is an exceptionally large task. But once he realises that it is God telling him that he is supported and capable of such a task, he rises to the challenge.

How does God see you?

VICTORIA BYRNE

What do I magnify?

And Mary said: 'My soul glorifies the Lord and my spirit rejoices in God my Saviour, for he has been mindful of the humble state of his servant. From now on all generations will call me blessed.' (NIV)

I'm fascinated by the virgin Mary's response to God's calling, which is so utterly free from doubt in God's plan. What impressive faith she had, not in her own human resources, but in God's love and mindfulness of her. Whereas in yesterday's passage, Gideon thinks: surely I can't because I'm the least; Mary thinks: God knows I'm the least, yet this is his plan. Mary's trust in God helps her marvel at God's plan, instead of picking it apart, because she recalls him as the faithful promise-keeper. She remembers what God has already brought her people through, and the way he has treated those who thought themselves strong in their own eyes. Those recollections strengthen her.

For Mary, the most extraordinary miracle of all has just occurred: she is pregnant by the Holy Spirit. It would be reasonable to think she had countless questions about the future and doubts about what is to come. Maybe all the future unknowns paled in comparison with the miraculous truth that what God had promised was already growing inside her. Her miraculous pregnancy must have been far beyond her expectations of how God worked.

She had tangible evidence of his miraculous power, but she shows how familiar she is with God's loving character by reacting with trust and worship. She knows what God is like, and benefits from him by dwelling on what he is like, rather than focusing on her doubts.

When I hit a challenge, of considerably smaller import than Mary's, I would do well to recall that this is not the first time he has led nervous women through difficult times. I could stand to trust him more, my God who has for millennia led his people into his promises.

Considering your own calling, how might you praise God?

VICTORIA BYRNE

Uncovering the real problem

After fasting forty days and forty nights, he was hungry. The tempter came to him and said, 'If you are the Son of God, tell these stones to become bread.' (NIV)

I've been thinking about whether Jesus ever wrestled with doubt. We know the devil tempted him, that Jesus did not sin and that he had free will, being fully human and fully God. When the devil said to Jesus, 'If you are the Son of God, tell these stones to become bread,' what doubt was being offered to Jesus? Was this a challenge over Jesus' motivations for creative miracles, or was it an invitation to prove to the devil that he was the Son of God?

Hidden beneath any temptation is potentially a much greater invitation to doubt. While Jesus fought a battle over his power to satisfy his hunger, could he have been battling the worry that he was not the Son of God?

When God's truth is being attacked, doubts can multiply. The devil may tempt us by saying something like: 'If you were really God's beloved child, then you wouldn't be in any pain!' If we accept the question's premise and the pain persists, then we may quietly conclude that we are not loved by God. One doubt leads to another, but looking beyond the doubt we can see the truth of God's love.

That happened yesterday, when a seemingly benign thought came to mind: 'Shouldn't I be sharing inspiring photos like my friend does?' That quickly led towards self-condemning thoughts: 'Perhaps I would be doing that if I were really creative; I guess I'm not.' How quickly feelings of power-lessness creep in!

God prompted me to challenge the thought. At once I could acknowledge how hard my friend works at creating those photos and how generous and varied are God's gifts to us all. With that, I could give thanks for my friend's gifts, and for mine too.

Think back over yesterday: was there any hidden challenge in something that bothered you?

VICTORIA BYRNE

Craftsmanship

'I have filled him with the Spirit of God, with wisdom, with understanding, with knowledge and with all kinds of skills – to make artistic designs for work in gold, silver and bronze, to cut and set stones, to work in wood, and to engage in all kinds of crafts.' (NIV)

If you have ever known the fear of the blank page ahead, you have known doubt. Is that the same as doubting God? Is it self-doubt? I would say it's some of both. Our passage today gives me encouragement that God who created the cosmos is concerned for the creative challenges we face, and all challenges are creative. Whether you are leading a team, being the helper or doing overtly 'creative' work, God is ready to meet the practical challenges of your day ahead. We all have natural skills, but God filled us with his Spirit when we believed in him, so he is working through you as he did with these craftsmen.

We've probably all stood in a cathedral, or even a simple chapel, and sensed the worship expressed in the very fabric of the sanctuary. When God commissioned these works and the people to do them, he gave them the means to carry out his desires. The men appointed to oversee the creation of the tabernacle furnishings were already known as skilled in their craft, but God also filled them with his Spirit to accomplish the work. I love that the different crafts are named. God enjoys the varied and beautiful ways we can create places that speak of his glory.

Yesterday I met my team to plan the preaching programme for our weekly service. We each prayerfully listened beforehand to see what God wanted. We met and shared our suggestions. Wonderfully, one person had a series of subjects; another had one angle that had been overlooked; the others had ideas that confirmed the general direction. One person might plan the preaching programme more quickly, but it glorifies God and strengthens our community when we unite in inviting God's anointing and guidance.

'For we are his workmanship, created in Christ Jesus for good works, which God prepared beforehand that we should walk in them' (Ephesians 2:10, NKJV).

VICTORIA BYRNE

Doubts about the way forward

This brought Paul and Barnabas into sharp dispute and debate with them. So Paul and Barnabas were appointed, along with some other believers, to go up to Jerusalem to see the apostles and elders about this question. (NIV)

This week I faced many big questions and doubts. As I write, my church is making plans to restart in-person services while keeping the best of the innovations made during the lockdowns of the past year. My colleagues wanted to hear what my ministry was going to do, to inform their wider preparations. I felt the need to have all the decisions made quickly. Yet God prevented me from meeting my closest colleague, so we could not agree our position on every possible plan in time for the meeting. All I could do was to acknowledge what we did know so far and to be transparent about what was still unclear about the road ahead.

It's fun to reflect on the disciples and apostles figuring out how to proceed with an even greater set of unknowns. They had a lot of 'blank pages' ahead of them. They were literally writing the book on godly conduct for the early church. They brought their disagreements to the meeting, looked at what God was doing as a sign of what he wanted, ensured their plan was anchored in scripture and made a roadmap, one step forward at a time.

Praise God, my meeting was truly fruitful; we each brought pieces of the puzzle and together we dispelled each other's fears and doubts. Despite my earnest wish to be sure of what was right from the very beginning, the point was to meet with colleagues and figure it out as a team. Despite our doubts about God's plans, this is an exciting time in the church's history, when we have reached the very edge of the church's planning calendar and need new schedules and new ways of working. May God help us collaborate fruitfully in looking to the future.

Read Psalm 107 for emotional descriptions of God rescuing his people many times when they were full of doubt.

VICTORIA BYRNE

Doubt and the visibility of God

'I will ask the Father, and he will give you another advocate to help you and be with you forever – the Spirit of truth. The world cannot accept him, because it neither sees him nor knows him. But you know him, for he lives with you.' (NIV)

I've been pondering biblical accounts of vivid interactions with God and considering how such an interaction could wipe away a person's doubts. Think of Moses speaking face to face with God, or the disciples apprenticed to Jesus for three years. When God gave the Israelites orders (Exodus 20), he even put it in writing!

Did these interactions really resolve people's doubts? I feel encouraged that the Israelites didn't find it easy to follow God even though Moses met with God face to face. As I pondered how Jesus prepared the believers to flourish even after his physical time on earth, I feel a connection to their need to adjust to a God who is present but invisible. In moments of personal doubt, it's easy for us to wish God would just make it all clear; would tell us his thoughts, his instructions. Yet even during Jesus' physical presence, the disciples had to wrestle with doubt and come to their own understanding of him as God. Thus it takes some time for Peter to come to the acknowledgement that Jesus is the Messiah (Matthew 16:13–17). Isn't it comforting to know that this was not an instant revelation even for one of Jesus' closest disciples?

With the resurrection of Jesus, God promised his permanent availability to us and put his Spirit of truth in us. As we collaborate on these daily reflections as writers and readers, we participate in a great conversation with God that has been happening since Jesus ascended into heaven. We will grow as we seek greater understanding of God's character and his daily revelation. Today's scripture reminds us again that though Jesus is not physically present, his Spirit continues to reveal truth.

What was the Holy Spirit showing you as you read today's passage?

VICTORIA BYRNE

Why, God?

At noon, darkness came over the whole land until three in the afternoon. And at three in the afternoon Jesus cried out in a loud voice, *'Eloi, Eloi, lema sabachthani'*? (which means 'My God, my God, why have you forsaken me?'). (NIV)

Has anyone ever asked you something that took you back to square one? My husband asked a great question today: was Jesus doubting when he asked God, 'Why have you forsaken me?'

Is doubt a sin? I thought so; surely that's why we have to work to overcome it. Or is it one of life's regular challenges, a 'maintenance' task? Do I presume to suggest Jesus was wrong and the Father had not really abandoned him?

Why would the Father abandon anyone? Isaiah 6:5 shows that the sinful cannot stand the presence of God's blazing goodness without God's help. But Jesus had not sinned; he was crucified through false accusation, improper trial and the people's will. So why God's abandonment? I feel like I'm entering Jesus' puzzlement for the first time.

I wondered if God took his presence away or Jesus just felt like he did. Perhaps the Father turned away in pain, because in that moment his Son was carrying the pain of all our sins. Was Jesus doubting the Father's attention to him? This feels like something I have not yet fully understood. When Jesus died, God forgave all sin, so that believers now have the privilege of being in God's permanent presence if we trust him. We do not need to understand every last detail for that to be true.

When we suffer and pain is close, we have our doubts and God's resolution can seem very far away. My feeling is that Jesus at least came close to that doubt, even though he had perfect faith that God had a plan (Luke 1:31–33).

Many hymns, songs and anthems engage with God's victory over doubt, sin and death, and conclude with the joy of God's presence. Which songs inspire you?

VICTORIA BYRNE

Overcoming

Then I heard a loud voice in heaven say: 'Now have come the salvation and the power and the kingdom of our God, and the authority of his Messiah… They triumphed over [the accuser] by the blood of the Lamb and by the word of their testimony.' (NIV)

During the Covid-19 lockdown, I was particularly aware that when I heard other people talking about what God had recently done, it scattered any gathering clouds of fear and doubt and I was put at ease. I work for a church, and you might think that faith in God's power and goodness is a given for church workers, but we need reminders of God's presence, power and goodness as much as anyone. Working closely with the church, I can access those stories more easily than when I worked in a secular company. The joy of the Bible is that we can all access and share that encouragement from the Bible and from other believers.

Every week in our staff meeting we have a chance to bear witness to what God has done that week and be strengthened against any doubts we might feel. Perhaps we've seen a problem solved even more neatly than we could have imagined. One colleague told us recently that they arrived late for school and observed a new family arrive at the school gates, mid-term, late and flustered. With anti-Covid measures in place, the mother could only wave their child into her new school and leave her to it. My friend was just nearing home when she saw the same parent. Finding that they were neighbours, she discovered the family needed furniture, orientation and friendship, and was able to help. She also learned the parent was Christian, had already watched our services online, and that very morning had asked God for urgent help.

My faith was boosted at hearing of God's cleverness and kindness. We know from Revelation 12:11 that evil is overcome by Jesus' sacrifice and by the testimony of believers. Bearing witness to how our invisible God has blessed us has powerful effects.

Are there communities or relationships in your life where you can share testimonies of God's recent care, to overcome doubt together?

VICTORIA BYRNE

The good wrestle

Jacob replied, 'I will not let you go unless you bless me.' The man asked him, 'What is your name?' 'Jacob,' he answered. Then the man said, 'Your name will no longer be Jacob, but Israel, because you have struggled with God and with humans and have overcome.' (NIV)

Jacob's wrestle through the night reminds me of wrestling with God about our doubts. Doubts have their place in our journey of faith. We're wrong if we think we've always got it right. I am cautious of any fellow believer who claims to always know what God is saying. We need to be accountable to one another and God, which is why comprehensively reading the Bible is such good training.

The right way is not always obvious. Church history is littered with the wrongs of people who convinced themselves of God's approval, such as clergymen who did not condemn the atrocity of slavery and even kept slaves themselves. We read those accounts and wonder how they ignored God's compassion for the captives, or God's love of free will.

There lies the key – God gives us all free will. If he removed every doubt from us, we would lose freedom and the power to disobey, but also the value of good deeds, of worship. So working through doubt can be complex: God rarely makes the answers obvious. Every act of overcoming doubt has its valuable wrestling with God. The answer is to do it with him.

I notice the lows and the highs as I review my life of faith. The wrestling threw up big questions: how God would answer righteous prayers for people I loved; how a fellow believer could claim to hear from God and yet seem so unloving with it; God's attitude towards me when I face criticism. These were times of anguish, but having wrestled with those doubts about God's character, will or attitude towards me, that's when I have also been most attentive to him. I look back on a painful time of wrestling, and I treasure those moments when God was powerfully present.

'Though the Lord is great, he cares for the humble, but he keeps his distance from the proud' (Psalm 138:6, NLT).

VICTORIA BYRNE

A time for everything

Claire Musters writes:

This famous passage from Ecclesiastes, often attributed to Solomon, is regularly read out at funerals. But how much do we really understand it – apart from the overriding message that God ordains when things happen?

To put this passage into the context of the whole book, it was written around 935BC, and it appears Solomon (or whoever the 'Teacher' was) was looking back over his life and sharing the lessons he learned through years of struggle. If it *was* Solomon, he may have had riches and power and been given wisdom by God, but he still made mistakes. Ultimately, he concluded that there is no meaning to be found in money, pleasure, work or knowledge – it can only be found in God.

Chapter 3 is part of a section within Ecclesiastes which shows that God has a purpose and a plan for his people. Our passage focuses on the cycle of life and begins: 'There is a time for everything, and a season for every activity under the heavens' (v. 1, NIV). Our lives are made up of so many elements: circumstances, seasons, the people we meet, the places we live and visit. So often we don't see how they all fit together.

My husband was once given a prophetic word about how his life was a tapestry – he was only seeing all the messy bits at the back, but God was creating a beautiful picture that one day he would see and understand. That is the essence of what is being said here – there is an ordained time for everything in the universe that God has set in motion. We might not understand it all, and we can look at the paradoxes of life and be confused or angered, but God has 'made everything beautiful in its time. He has also set eternity in the human heart; yet no one can fathom what God has done from beginning to end' (v. 11).

The secret to peace, we are told, is through accepting this and learning to live with eternity in mind. The difficult times we will face are not glossed over, but they sit alongside beautiful ones – we need to be prepared for both.

The verses we are concentrating on are written as poetry. Each line refers to opposite activities that occur in our lives. Some can easily be grouped together, such as killing/healing and love/hate, but others are more ambiguous, reflecting how life is complex. Let's take a closer look.

Life's framework

A time to be born and a time to die, a time to plant and a time to uproot. (NIV)

Our lives are bookmarked at either end by our birth and death. Right at the start of this passage we encounter the big picture, and yet our life on earth is simply part of our eternal existence.

We didn't ask to be born – it was God who knit us together (see Psalm 139:13). This reminds us that we are connected to something – and someone – far greater than ourselves. And, death, too, touches us all. It may seem scary and difficult, and as our bodies age and decay, we experience first-hand the harsh effect of the fall (watching my mum suffer as her health deteriorated was one of the most perplexing parts of my own life). And yet Jesus has made a way for us to enjoy resurrection life. We can learn to speak openly about death, but also about the hope of everlasting life.

Just as there is a cycle to the life of a plant, so too there is with our lives. Seeds are sown, fruit is picked, flowers die, crops are harvested and ground is given time to lay fallow in order to recover; bulbs are uprooted and protected over winter in greenhouses, then replanted in the springtime. All of this speaks to me of God's care for us in the seasons of our lives. Sometimes we feel like we have just been planted into a new place or purpose. At other times we may experience the gardener's pruning shears (see John 15), and there are winter seasons where it seems he is allowing purposes in our lives to lay dormant. In each season, his hand is moulding and shaping us. In fact, times of new birth involve pain too. It is uncomfortable; it involves change, and yet God is in the business of 'making everything new' (Revelation 21:5).

Reflect back over different seasons in your life – times of winter as well as those of new life. Ask God to reveal to you the new thing that he created in each change that he has brought to your mind.

CLAIRE MUSTERS

Killing what separates us

A time to kill and a time to heal, a time to tear down and a time to build. (NIV)

This verse can make us hugely uncomfortable. We don't like the imagery of killing – nor the fact that we read about it so much in the Old Testament. So much killing occurs at the hands of God's people – and God himself (see, for example, Judges 3:28–30). This can be difficult to get our heads around, particularly as we know God is 'gracious and compassionate, slow to anger and rich in love' (Psalm 145:8).

We need to view all this through the lens of Jesus. Before his death and resurrection, the killing of animals through sacrifice was the blood atonement necessary for God's people to keep in communion with him (see Leviticus 1 for an example of God's instructions on this). But we live in the time after Jesus' once-and-for-all blood sacrifice, which Hebrews 9:11–28 explains in the light of the Old Testament sacrifices (a really helpful passage).

What we do need to continue to kill, however, is anything that separates us from our loving heavenly Father. We see this type of language in Colossians 3:5: 'Put to death, therefore, whatever belongs to your earthly nature: sexual immorality, impurity, lust, evil desires and greed, which is idolatry.' Later on in that passage it talks of bearing with and forgiving one another (v. 13); that approach brings healing and harmony to relationships.

The original word used for 'heal' in Ecclesiastes is *raphe* – God calls himself the healer in Exodus 15:26, and Jesus did many healing miracles out of compassion. He is still in the business of tending to wounds today. Sometimes he does this in a way we find difficult – for instance, as the second part of this verse indicates, there are times when a stripping back is needed in order to bring about something new.

Take some time to thank Jesus for the healing that comes through his death, then consider how he is building your life today. Are there things that need tearing down in order for new things to be constructed well?

CLAIRE MUSTERS

Releasing our tears and joy

A time to weep and a time to laugh, a time to mourn and a time to dance. (NIV)

This verse became much more poignant to me after my mum went to be with Jesus. In my grief, I spent a lot of time sitting with the story of Jesus raising Lazarus from the dead (found in John 11). It was the shortest verse in the Bible, 'Jesus wept' (v. 35), that spoke to me most. Despite Jesus knowing that he was going to raise Lazarus, he not only felt Mary and Martha's grief, but also experienced deep emotion himself.

We can be concerned about showing any negative emotion in church, but Jesus wasn't worried about crying among the mourners in what was a very public place. We too can be free to weep and mourn when we need to. Not only that, but also Jesus weeps alongside us and holds us, comforting us as we do so. Tears release something in us. I have had many moments recently when I haven't been able to hold back the tears and I have felt that God knew I needed that release. In fact, the Bible gives us a language for doing so – lament.

We also need one another in our loss – in biblical times, mourning was much more of a community experience. Dancing was too, as we can see when David took the ark back to Jerusalem (2 Samuel 6). And after God had delivered the Israelites from Egypt, both Moses and Miriam wrote songs of thanks and there was much dancing (Exodus 15:20).

I am challenged by Jeremiah 31:4: 'Again you will… go out to dance with the joyful.' I am quite a reserved person and, while I am not advocating being overly flamboyant when it is not in my (or your) nature, I do wonder whether we fully embrace joy and celebration in our lives.

Take some time to think about whether you feel free to express your emotions openly before God – not only your lament but also exuberant joy. Ask him to help you if you find one (or both) difficult.

CLAIRE MUSTERS

Being together – and apart

A time to scatter stones and a time to gather them, a time to embrace and a time to refrain from embracing. (NIV)

The idea of scattering and gathering is one that reminds me of the way the gospel was spread in the early church. The disciples in those days would have been more familiar with the imagery used than we are today – indeed they lived with the threat of stoning as persecution hit the church. But it was through this that the scattering of people, and the message of Jesus' resurrection, happened. God works through both scattering and gathering. We see in scripture that people gathered for a purpose (often to hear God's word – see Mark 2:2; Acts 13:44).

I was struck afresh by what it says about gathering in Esther's story. When her Uncle Mordecai challenged her that perhaps she was placed in the palace 'for such a time as this' (Esther 4:14), she asked him to 'gather together all the Jews who are in Susa, and fast for me' (v. 16). We gather together to worship in our churches – this is a great challenge to actively support one another in our daily lives and in the spiritual battles we may face.

One of the battles we have faced in recent times is the Covid-19 pandemic. It's a stark example of a time when it was necessary to refrain from embracing. But there is a wider concept about boundaries within relationships here too. There will be moments when we are to welcome and embrace – and others when it is necessary to have a little distance or space. Learning the wisdom of that can be difficult, particularly as opening our hearts to others is a risky business, but one we are called to as Christians. When someone else hurts us, we are able to take that hurt to Jesus, but if we are repeatedly hurt, it might be time to seek wisdom for the relationship.

Thank God for the way that he gathers and scatters us with purpose, even when we may find the process difficult. Ask him to help you support those around you well and conduct your relationships wisely.

CLAIRE MUSTERS

When to hold on, when to let go

A time to search and a time to give up, a time to keep and a time to throw away. (NIV)

This verse reminds me of three of Jesus' parables from Luke 15: the lost sheep (vv. 1–7), the lost coins (vv. 8–10) and the lost son (vv. 11–32). In the first two stories, Jesus reveals how he constantly pursues us and rejoices when we are found. The parables also teach us the importance of not giving up – and yet the third reveals that there *is* a time when we need to let go.

How hard that must have been for the prodigal's father. When he asked for his inheritance, the son was basically saying he wished his father were dead. His father continued to love him, but also allowed him to walk away. The son squandered his inheritance 'in wild living' (v. 13). It was then that he realised the true treasure he had at home and returned. How many times do we run after the wrong things, ignoring those that are helpful? (When I'm exhausted, I can pick 'easy fixes' like TV and a glass of wine over spending time in my Father's presence.)

There are also times when God asks us to keep hold of difficult things (such as challenging situations that are teaching us perseverance and growing our character). But he also nudges us when it is time to let go – perhaps of a ministry we love – to give others room to develop. We need to look to God rather than culture or the opinion of others for instruction on this.

We hear his wisdom through prayer, reading his word, a 'quickening' inside as the Holy Spirit guides, and conversations and prayer with mature Christians. I am reminded of Isaiah 30:21: 'Whether you turn to the right or to the left, your ears will hear a voice behind you, saying, "This is the way; walk in it."'

Lord, help me to listen out for your voice over and above all others today, and to learn when I need to persevere in pursuing a relationship or situation – and when you are telling me to let go. Amen

CLAIRE MUSTERS

Bringing peace

A time to tear and a time to mend, a time to be silent and a time to speak. (NIV)

The Hebrew word translated as 'tear' here comes from the root *qara*, which is often used in the Old Testament in relation to grief and loss. The tearing of clothes was part of the mourning process. Job 'tore his robe' (Job 1:20). When his friends heard about his afflictions, they went to offer comfort. They began well, also tearing their robes and mourning alongside him. They then simply sat and said nothing (Job 2:12–13).

This is a great example of knowing when to stay silent. So often we feel the need to explain away problems or offer advice to those who are suffering, when all they need is our companionship so that they do not feel alone. It was when Job's friends opened their mouths that they angered God (Job 42:7). We need to practise the art of remaining silent, but also know when it is right to speak out against injustice and oppression (Proverbs 31:8–9). As Proverbs 18:21 puts it so well: 'The tongue has the power of life and death.' We can mend or tear down with our words – let us be those who bring peace.

I am not a needlewoman: I can sew on a button and mend a small tear, but I am fascinated by what others can make. God himself fashioned together garments for Adam and Eve to cover over their shame (Genesis 3:21). Jesus was stripped naked and hung on the cross in order to cover over our shame once and for all, and, as he died, 'the curtain of the temple was torn in two from top to bottom' (Matthew 27:51). Hebrews 10:20 explains that he opened up a way for us to reach the Father through 'the curtain, that is, his body'.

It is a bold prayer, but we can continue to ask Jesus to tear down anything in our lives that separates us from God. Why not take some time to talk to him about this today?

CLAIRE MUSTERS

Love God and others, fight injustice

A time to love and a time to hate, a time for war and a time for peace. (NIV)

Surely as Christians we are not meant to hate? Or go to war? And yet the Old Testament is full of bloodshed, as God fights on behalf of his people, often miraculously slaughtering their enemies (see, for example, 2 Chronicles 20). While we live the other side of Jesus' sacrifice, there are things that we are meant to hate and go to war against – including our own sin (as we saw on Monday).

We have also seen how the Bible teaches us to stand against injustice. Micah 6:8 exhorts us 'to act justly and to love mercy and to walk humbly with your God'. That verse always challenges me to ask: are there areas in my life where I've chosen comfort over social justice? Perhaps my shopping choices are actually helping to fuel an unjust system at their source. We need to ensure that *all* parts of our lives are revealing the love of God. This includes not only our day-to-day interactions with those around us (important as those are, because they reveal Jesus – as he said in John 17:20–23), but also our behaviour and lifestyle choices. And, as Hebrews 12:14 exhorts us, we are also to 'make every effort to live in peace with everyone'.

As our exploration of the poetic section of Ecclesiastes 3 comes to an end, it has revealed how complex the world is. There are no easy answers to many of our questions, and yet, we *can* find meaning in our lives despite that. So much is out of our hands, and it is important to recognise that life can be a struggle. Yet, when we recognise that God is ultimately in control, we can 'walk humbly' in step with him throughout our lives.

Take some time to thank God that he set the earth into motion and has ordained each one of your days. Bring before him any situation that you are finding difficult or confusing. Finally, ask him for his continued guidance.

CLAIRE MUSTERS

Blessings from the psalms

Jackie Harris writes:

Who doesn't love the psalms? Probably the best loved and most read book in the Old Testament, Psalms covers a wide variety of themes. Some of the psalms call the community to praise God for who he is and what he has done. Others present important truths. Some express great heartache and sorrow or urgent pleas for the Lord to act. And then there are personal prayers of confession or thanksgiving. Together, they express all the hopes, joys, sorrows, doubts, disappointments and aspirations of the human heart. No wonder many of us turn to the psalms to help us pray through different challenges and experiences.

They also teach us a lot about the character of God, especially his faith-fulness, care and provision for his people. The psalmists knew God to be there for them, shouldering their burdens, guiding their feet, taking their hand and holding them close in times of trouble. But what many of us love most is the honesty of the psalmists. They were not afraid to be open about their fears and failings or their bewilderment when they didn't understand what was happening or felt God was far away. They show us that we don't have to present a sanitised version of ourselves to God; we can come as we are: red-faced and angry, awkward and penitent, distressed or mournful… And as we reflect on their words, we are encouraged by their faith, trust and honesty to seek God's counsel, forgiveness and comfort for ourselves.

Over the next few days, we invite you to read a selection of psalms that have played a part in our own journeys of faith or hold a special place in our hearts. Some have been an encouragement at a particular time, some hold particular remembrances and others are scriptures we return to again and again. We pray they will speak to you, too, of God who is with us always, whatever our circumstances, and who cares for us.

Let's begin with a prayer of David: 'Show me your ways, Lord, teach me your paths. Guide me in your truth and teach me, for you are God my Saviour, and my hope is in you all day long' (Psalm 25:4–5, NIV).

Pleasant places

The boundary lines have fallen for me in pleasant places; surely I have a delightful inheritance. (NIV)

Before I moved to Britain, I held images of this land that were informed by culture – such as the sweeping countryside featured in the BBC adaptation of *Pride and Prejudice*. But when I moved here, newly married to my English husband, I not only glimpsed the glories of cathedrals and thatched cottages and enjoyed the gift of abiding friendship, but I also started to understand some of the challenges we face in the not-so-always United Kingdom.

And yet I could echo with David his song: 'Lord, you alone are my portion and my cup; you make my lot secure. The boundary lines have fallen for me in pleasant places; surely I have a delightful inheritance' (Psalm 16:5–6). I thought a lot about these boundary lines, sometimes considering them as my husband and I drove along the hedgerows dividing up the countryside or when I saw all the fenced-in gardens, so different to the open layout I knew from America.

I began to realise that God gives me freedom within the constraints. Those boundary lines have given me space over the years to explore my identity as a wife, mother, editor, author, speaker, retreat leader and spiritual director. Who knows what my life would have looked like had I stayed Stateside, but here God has given me the opportunities to develop in wonderful ways. I might bristle against the accepted mode of humour (I still don't understand irony) and long to see family and friends across the Pond, but with David I can say that God has given me a delightful inheritance, that 'my heart is glad and my tongue rejoices' (v. 9).

Wherever your boundary lines have fallen, trust that with God at your side, you can rest secure in him.

Lord, you make known to me the path of life, and I love to walk it with you. Fill me with joy in your presence, and help me to rest secure in you. Amen
AMY BOUCHER PYE

An honest outpouring

My wounds fester and are loathsome because of my sinful folly. (NIV)

I am pretty sure this psalm will not be an obvious favourite for many, and yet it holds a place in my heart for a very particular reason: it helped me understand that I could speak to God honestly at any time in my life.

I have gone on a huge journey in recent years learning more about giving space to lament – mainly due to grief and other painful circumstances. I have discovered that in the psalms we are shown how to voice our complaints, fears and upsets – alongside our worship. However, the first time a psalm spoke to me – I mean totally disarmed me because it described *exactly* how I was feeling – was when I read Psalm 38 years ago.

I had made some huge mistakes and found myself living back with my parents in my late 20s, not knowing if my marriage could be saved or whether I had a home, church or job anymore. I was utterly wretched due to my own sin and its consequences. I didn't know how or what to pray… that is, until I discovered this psalm. It became the prayer I prayed to God – and I meant every… single… word.

Knowing David's backstory, which resonated with my own,* I was so reassured by his honest pleading with God, and it set me on a course of laying everything bare before my heavenly Father – including all of the emotions I was still struggling with.

I think this psalm is such a great encouragement to us all that we need never hide from God out of guilt or shame; it is precisely in those times that we need him most.

Claire tells more of this story in Taking Off the Mask *and* Grace-Filled Marriage *(written alongside her husband). Both are published by Authentic Media.*

Lord, I thank you that the Bible includes psalms such as this one, which teach us that it is okay to be honest about our failings and mixed motives. Help me draw near to you daily, however I am feeling. Amen

CLAIRE MUSTERS

God our refuge

God is our refuge and strength, an ever-present help in trouble. Therefore we will not fear, though the earth give way and the mountains fall into the heart of the sea… He says, 'Be still, and know that I am God.' (NIV)

I can still remember the day when my world was turned upside down. It was a normal school day. I went downstairs to get my breakfast along with my five-year-old and two-year-old. I turned to walk back towards the front door and up the stairs, and that was when I noticed it – an envelope – peeking out of the letterbox.

'That's odd!' I thought. The postman normally comes later in the day. I grabbed the envelope, thinking it would be junk mail, ripped it open and skimmed the inside. It was something about the railway. I assumed they were closing the crossing near our house again. But then something jumped out at me: a small phrase that set off alarm bells – 'The government may need to buy some or all of your property.'

At that point, my mind started racing and I read the letter again fully, realising that it was regarding HS2, the new high-speed railway, which they had now decided would go right through my brand-new home. Thus started a two-year journey of stress and anguish, leading us to selling our home to the government and moving elsewhere.

During those first few days and weeks of chaos, when journalists swarmed our tiny estate, politicians appeared outside my home and neighbours turned against neighbours, I took great comfort from this psalm. The meaning of the word 'refuge' – to be sheltered from danger – really resonated with me. I pictured this little bubble or cocoon that me and God would sit in together, away from the chaos in my life at that point. The world could collapse around me, but me and God were okay together. He would give me all the strength I needed to get through.

What do you need refuge from now? Picture yourself sitting in a safe bubble with God where the trouble that surrounds you cannot reach you. Ask God to help you be still and embrace that refuge with him.

RACHEL RIDLER

In the desert place

You, God, are my God, earnestly I seek you; I thirst for you, my whole being longs for you, in a dry and parched land where there is no water. (NIV)

'A dry and parched land where there is no water.' David wrote this psalm while he was in a wilderness. He remembers the power and glory he experienced in the sanctuary. Even though his situation is dreadful, he draws strength from reminding himself of the truth, that God's everlasting love is better than life. Whatever happens, he will not withhold his praise.

This psalm celebrates the choice that David makes to praise God in all circumstances. Even at night he remembers God. He doesn't toss and turn, eaten up by fears and anxieties over his situation. Instead, he disciplines his mind to contemplate the God whose love is better than life. He overcomes his fear by focusing on the one whose love drives out fear. There is no room for fear in love.

Immediately after his baptism, Jesus was led by the Spirit into the desert, where he fasted and prayed for 40 days. The desert is often the place for profound God-encounters.

This is a special psalm to me. I was devastated when my sister and best friend, Judy, died at age 37. I was in a dry and parched land where there was no water – but God was there with me. He helped me focus on the faith displayed by David in this powerful psalm. He drew me to it, again and again, and as he enabled my lips to praise him, he comforted my soul. 'Because you are my help, I sing in the shadow of your wings' (v. 7).

Unable to sleep last night, I got up and had an hour-long God-encounter. I returned to bed refreshed and at peace. Whenever I encounter challenging circumstances, I return to this psalm. If you find yourself in a desert today, cling to God and he will uphold you.

Ours is a faithful, loving Lord, who never, ever forsakes us. Praise him always, whatever your circumstances. 'Because your love is better than life, my lips will glorify you' (v. 3).

MICHELE D. MORRISON

It's not fair!

When I tried to understand all this, it troubled me deeply till I entered the sanctuary of God; then I understood their final destiny. (NIV)

What I particularly like about this psalm is its honesty: it expresses real doubt and pain. I remember reading it once when I was feeling particularly sorry for myself: things appeared to be going a lot better for other people than for me, and I was fed up. You can see why this psalm resonated!

The issues the psalmist raises are timeless: how can we reconcile our belief in a faithful, powerful, just God with the evil we see all around us? The psalmist describes people he knew behaving badly and seeming not only to get away with it but also to prosper. Indeed, many were wealthier, healthier and less troubled than the psalmist, who, as a result, was beginning to question whether there was any point in serving God.

Are we as honest with the Lord about our doubts as this psalmist, or do we try not to think about our questions and sweep them under the carpet? Perhaps we feel uncomfortable talking to God about such things, thinking it disrespectful and so, instead, present a sanitised version of ourselves to God when we pray. But it was the psalmist's raw honesty in prayer that helped him: his whole attitude changed after he visited the sanctuary and brought his complaints to God.

This is so encouraging, for it shows us that all is not lost if we are struggling to trust God in difficult circumstances. Faith is not something we summon up through our own efforts alone; it grows naturally as we come to God in our weaknesses and seek his help to see things his way and do what he wants. As Psalm 73 reflects, this means the least promising of circumstances can turn out to be real opportunities for growth if we are just honest in prayer.

Spend time being honest with God about the things that are troubling you and any doubts and questions you have about your faith. Ask God for help to trust him and to see things from his perspective.

CAROLINE FLETCHER

Remembering God's goodness

Return to your rest, my soul, for the Lord has been good to you. For you, Lord, have delivered me from death, my eyes from tears, my feet from stumbling, that I may walk before the Lord in the land of the living. (NIV)

In this psalm, as with many of the psalms, the writer speaks honestly to God, giving thanks and praise after surviving a season of pain and anguish. We do not know exactly what has happened to this person, but their testimony is that God has been good despite it all. God is recognised as the one who has heard their cries for help and has brought them through their difficulties. This psalm invites us to trust the God who has proven to be faithful to the writer and inspires us to believe that this same God might also be faithful in our lives.

If we are honest, it can be difficult to trust God. Sometimes believing and hoping feels too costly, especially when we have felt disappointed in the past. God is beyond our full understanding; we do not always know what God is doing and sometimes he does not do what we hope for. For these reasons, our souls are not always at rest. Can we be comforted by the words of this psalm even while death is close to us, our eyes are filled with tears and our feet stumble?

We are reminded here that despair will pass and, in the end, we will be able to look back and see the goodness of God who delivers us, dries our eyes and steadies our feet. This can be impossible to imagine when we are in the midst of difficulty, but as a friend of mine once said, 'Try not to judge God in the middle!' Remembering the goodness of God is not always at the forefront of our minds in the midst of distress, but it is a sure antidote to the despair that tempts us to deny the nature of God, which is goodness and love.

Look back over your life and the lives of those you know. Where are the signs of God's faithfulness and deliverance? Allow them to encourage you as you face the challenges that are now present in your life.

SELINA STONE

Planting hope

Those who sow with tears will reap with songs of joy. Those who go out weeping, carrying seed to sow, will return with songs of joy, carrying sheaves with them. (NIV)

Years ago, I was in a team leading a particularly emotional conference that wound up with 48 hours of intensive collaboration. It was a successful weekend, but there were tears as some of us were taxed beyond our resources. I remember recalling this psalm as I walked out into the fresh air, and I repeated its words while acknowledging my own relief, exhaustion and satisfaction.

This psalm is a tearful, poetic rush of longing and hope. The wonderful footnotes of The Passion Translation explain that Psalm 126 is the prayer-song of those Israelites who have returned to Jerusalem from exile. While they rejoice at being reunited with their homes and the temple in which they feel closest to God, they have not yet received the full answer to their prayers, because they await the return of the other Israelites still in exile.

When God gives us hope for something, it can mean frustration and longing, but also peace and expectation. We are in a world in which God has conquered evil, and yet we still need to live alongside it in our daily lives. God knows our need of hope. Paul writes, 'I pray that the eyes of your heart may be enlightened in order that you may know the hope to which he has called you, the riches of his glorious inheritance in his holy people' (Ephesians 1:18).

I am moved by such poetry and by the wonder of the harvest. The sowing is hard work, burying tiny seeds, and the fruition may take years. It takes hope to keep persevering, but God is faithful and one day we will see that it was all abundantly worth it.

'To him who is able to do immeasurably more than all we ask or imagine, according to his power that is at work within us, to him be glory in the church and in Christ Jesus' (Ephesians 3:20–21).

VICTORIA BYRNE

A call to unity

How wonderful, how beautiful, when brothers and sisters get along! It's like costly anointing oil flowing down head and beard, flowing down Aaron's beard, flowing down the collar of his priestly robes. It's like the dew on Mount Hermon flowing down the slopes of Zion. Yes, that's where God commands the blessing, ordains eternal life. (MSG)

I recall the many times after my hair had been washed and air-dried, my mother would direct me to sit on a stool in front of her. Armed with an extra-large comb, she would begin the arduous and time-consuming process of combing through my long hair (the latter being a traditional prerequisite for both male and female Sikhs).

After what seemed like an age of tugging and pulling, accompanied by the occasional shriek from me, my mother would then slowly and deliberately pour olive oil on top of my scalp. This was and still is the best conditioner ever! I recall the oil trickling down all over my head, with the occasional droplet falling onto my chemise (a top frequently worn by South Asian women and girls). My mother would follow this with a 'root to shoot' massage. I found this very ordinary ritual to be a profound blessing.

Within the ancient Near East, the custom of lavishly pouring special fragrant oil on the head of a guest after journeying through the heat of the day signified welcome, generosity and hospitality. This beautiful image is evoked in Psalm 133, where the oil trickles down over Aaron's beard and garments. It powerfully reflects the blessings bestowed by God *himself* wherever his people live in unity. Surely this is a foretaste of heaven!

Living in unity is not an empty phrase or optional extra. This psalm depicts God as being attracted to unity and conferring tangible blessings upon it. The psalm also challenges us to intentionally, as far as it depends on you and me, 'live out' tangible expressions of unity by taking whatever steps we can towards it, for example, apology, repentance, forgiveness and reconciliation.

How can you forge unity today?

CHAM KAUR MANN

Praise in the keeping-going

Praise the Lord, all you servants of the Lord who minister by night in the house of the Lord. Lift up your hands in the sanctuary and praise the Lord. May the Lord bless you from Zion, he who is the Maker of heaven and earth. (NIV)

A dark chapel, candlelit at altar and stalls. A friend and I hold candles, standing by the door to welcome people into the hushed sanctuary for night prayer.

It is late. I am tired. But my heart is full of the gift of knowing I'm where I'm meant to be – and that is enough to keep me standing. Keep me opening the door. Keep me providing candles and whispered answers to newcomers' questions. It is enough to keep me serving in the way that God has called me.

That evening, my heart was full. I was *tired* – so much so that I accidentally blew hot wax into my friend's face as we extinguished the candles (a fact he didn't reveal to me for months, and for which I'm still apologetic). Yet, despite such tiredness and injury, my heart was full. I praised God to choir's song and latecomers' arrivals.

Psalm 134 speaks to such moments of finding joy in the everyday task of keeping going in the way that God has called us.

Praise God, the psalmist sings, when you're awake in the dark doing the work you know to be good. Praise God when you serve in the night-time – the literal night-time, or the night-time of the soul when all things feel dark.

No matter what it is you're keeping going with, God sees your faithfulness and calls you to praise. That is not to say that you should 'just keep going' when you're in a situation that is damaging or that you need to change or leave. Rather, this psalm is for when you're doing good work in the place you know is right. In that place, keep going and keep praising. As you keep going, may the Lord bless you, he who made heaven and earth.

Call to mind times you've felt weary as you've just been keeping going. Ask God to draw alongside you, helping you to nevertheless give praise for them. Hold on to the promise of his blessing, as you keep walking in his way.

HANNAH FYTCHE

Fearfully and wonderfully made

I will praise You, for I am fearfully and wonderfully made; Marvellous are Your works, And that my soul knows very well. (NKJV)

This must be my favourite psalm. My mum taught me Psalm 139:14 in my early childhood – and what a beautiful treasure it is. I am made in the image of God (Genesis 1:27), fashioned with breath-taking wonder: my every fibre stamped with his fingerprint. Wow! Say it loud: *I am God's masterpiece.* It's the truth.

God, your creator, knows you inside and out. Before you were even born, he had encyclopedic knowledge of everything about you – yes, even before your body had begun to form and you were just a little fertilised egg! God had written the story of your life before it even began (v. 16).

During my childhood, I found solace and strength in these words – and I still do today. They have shaped the foundation of my identity. When I've been mistreated on the basis of my skin colour, I've come back to who God says I am. When the enemy whispers lies to me about my value and worth, I come back to these words. They change everything.

God's knowledge of your life didn't end when you started living it. He has 24/7 CCTV coverage of your every moment. Our Father promises never to leave nor forsake us, and he means it literally. He is a mind-reader too: he knows what we're about to say before our lips even shape the words.

I share in the awe that David expresses in every word of this psalm. *The Message* version aptly translates verse 17 like this: 'Your thoughts – how rare, how beautiful! God, I'll never comprehend them!'

When we are bowled over by God's majesty, it changes everything: how we see him, how we see ourselves and how we see others. For every person on this earth is fearfully and wonderfully made, fully known and fully loved, by the Almighty Creator.

Father God, I praise you because I am fearfully and wonderfully made in your image. I know this to be the full truth. Remind me, when I doubt my worth, of who I am because of who you are. Amen

RUTH AKINRADEWO

Picture God

The Lord is gracious and compassionate, slow to anger and rich in love. (NIV)

When you close your eyes and imagine God, what do you see? A.W. Tozer famously said: 'What comes to mind when you think about God is the most important thing about you.' It's important because what we truly believe about God will affect everything we do, the decisions we make and how we interpret what happens to us.

It came as rather a shock when I realised that despite all the wonderful things I knew about God, deep, deep down the image I had was of someone constantly tapping his feet or rolling his eyes in annoyance. It's an image that can still rear up from time to time, and these wonderful words from David help me to refocus on the truth.

In fact, these words from verse 8 echo how God describes himself to Moses when he met with him on Mount Sinai (Exodus 34:4–6). He is compassionate and gracious, abounding in love and faithfulness, and David has experienced this for himself. What he writes in this psalm is not a theoretical knowledge of God, but what David has seen and felt and known.

David rightly recognises God's majesty and power, but he also tells us that God is trustworthy, that he sustains those who fall or are burdened, and that he is righteous in his ways and kind in his deeds. He knows God as one who is always close, always ready to listen and always watching over him. No wonder David is moved to praise as he reflects on God's character and his goodness. May we too recognise the depth of God's love and care for us and know him as he is – gracious and compassionate, slow to anger and rich in love – in the deep places of our hearts.

If you have time, read through the whole psalm again and record what you learn about who God is and what he does. Which things about God are most precious to you? Which ones do you need to experience today?

JACKIE HARRIS

Enabling all ages to grow in faith

Anna Chaplaincy

Living Faith

Messy Church

Parenting for Faith

100 years of BRF

2022 is BRF's 100th anniversary! Look out for details of our special new centenary resources, a beautiful centenary rose and an online thanksgiving service that we hope you'll attend. This centenary year we're focusing on sharing the story of BRF, the story of the Bible – and we hope you'll share your stories of faith with us too.

Find out more at **brf.org.uk/centenary**.

To find out more about our work, visit

brf.org.uk

Sharing
the Story
since 1922

Each issue of *Day by Day with God* is available from Christian bookshops everywhere. Copies may also be available through your church book agent or from the person who distributes Bible reading notes in your church.

Alternatively you may obtain *Day by Day with God* on subscription direct from the publishers. There are two kinds of subscription:

Individual subscriptions
covering 3 issues for 4 copies or less, payable in advance
(including postage & packing).

To order, please complete the details on page 144 and return with the appropriate payment to: BRF, 15 The Chambers, Vineyard, Abingdon OX14 3FE

You can also use the form on page 144 to order a gift subscription for a friend.

Group subscriptions
covering 3 issues for 5 copies or more, sent to one UK address (post free).

Please note that the annual billing period for group subscriptions runs from 1 May to 30 April.

To order, please complete the details on page 143 and return with the appropriate payment to: BRF, 15 The Chambers, Vineyard, Abingdon OX14 3FE

You will receive an invoice with the first issue of notes.

All our Bible reading notes can be ordered online by visiting
brfonline.org.uk/collections/subscriptions

Day by Day with God is also available as
an app for Android, iPhone and iPad
brfonline.org.uk/collections/apps

Follow us on Instagram: **@daybydaywithgod**

All subscription enquiries should be directed to:
BRF, 15 The Chambers, Vineyard, Abingdon OX14 3FE
+44 (0)1865 319700 | **enquiries@brf.org.uk**

DBDWG0222

DAY BY DAY WITH GOD GROUP SUBSCRIPTION FORM

All our Bible reading notes can be ordered online by visiting
brfonline.org.uk/collections/subscriptions

The group subscription rate for *Day by Day with God* will be £14.55 per person until April 2023.

☐ I would like to take out a group subscription for _____ (quantity) copies.

☐ Please start my order with the September 2022 / January 2023 / May 2023* issue. I would like to pay annually/receive an invoice* with each edition of the notes. (*delete as appropriate)

Please do not send any money with your order. Send your order to BRF and we will send you an invoice.

Name and address of the person organising the group subscription:

Title _____ First name/initials _____ Surname _____

Address_____

_____ Postcode _____

Telephone _____ Email _____

Church_____

Name and address of the person paying the invoice if the invoice needs to be sent directly to them:

Title _____ First name/initials _____ Surname _____

Address_____

_____ Postcode _____

Telephone _____ Email _____

We will use your personal data to process this order. From time to time we may send you information about the work of BRF. Please contact us if you wish to discuss your mailing preferences **brf.org.uk/privacy**

Please return this form to:
BRF, 15 The Chambers, Vineyard, Abingdon OX14 3FE | **enquiries@brf.org.uk**

For terms and cancellation information, please visit **brfonline.org.uk/terms**.

Bible Reading Fellowship is a charity (233280) and company limited by guarantee (301324), registered in England and Wales

DAY BY DAY WITH GOD INDIVIDUAL/GIFT SUBSCRIPTION FORM

To order online, please visit **brfonline.org.uk/collections/subscriptions**

☐ I would like to give a gift subscription (please provide both names and addresses)

☐ I would like to take out a subscription myself (complete your name and address details only once)

Title _____ First name/initials _____ Surname _____

Address _____

_____ Postcode _____

Telephone _____ Email _____

Gift subscription name _____

Gift subscription address _____

_____ Postcode _____

Gift subscription (20 words max. or include your own gift card):

_____

_____

Please send *Day by Day with God* beginning with the September 2022 / January 2023 / May 2023 issue (*delete as appropriate*):

(*please tick box*)	UK	Europe	Rest of world
1-year subscription	☐ £18.30	☐ £26.25	☐ £30.15
2-year subscription	☐ £35.70	N/A	N/A

Optional donation to support the work of BRF £ _____

Total enclosed £ _____ (cheques should be made payable to 'BRF')

Please charge my MasterCard / Visa with £ _____

Card no. ☐☐☐☐ ☐☐☐☐ ☐☐☐☐ ☐☐☐☐

Expires end [M M] [Y Y]   Security code [☐ ☐ ☐]   Last 3 digits on the reverse of the card

We will use your personal data to process this order. From time to time we may send you information about the work of BRF. Please contact us if you wish to discuss your mailing preferences **brf.org.uk/privacy**

Please return this form to:

BRF, 15 The Chambers, Vineyard, Abingdon OX14 3FE | **enquiries@brf.org.uk**

For terms and cancellation information, please visit **brfonline.org.uk/terms**.

Bible Reading Fellowship is a charity (233280) and company limited by guarantee (301324), registered in England and Wales

DBDWG0222